Games/Hobbies $6-

GAMES
chess

D0848098

040321

HOW TO PLAY THE
ENDGAME IN CHESS

HOW TO PLAY THE
ENDGAME
IN CHESS

LEONARD BARDEN

THE BOBBS-MERRILL COMPANY, INC.
INDIANAPOLIS NEW YORK

Published in the United States by The Bobbs-Merrill Company, Inc.
Indianapolis New York
Published in Great Britain by William Collins Sons & Co. Ltd.

ISBN 0-672-52086-9
Library of Congress Catalog Card Number: 74-17685

Manufactured in Great Britain

First U.S. printing 1975

TO
PETER MORRISH
STEWART REUBEN
EDDIE PENN
DAVID EUSTACE
and other overworked British
chess organisers

CONTENTS

Introduction   9

PART ONE

BASIC ENDGAME TECHNIQUE

1 **The king in action**   15
   The king shepherds home passed pawns   16
   The king joins in an attack against the enemy king   20
   The king penetrates the enemy position and captures
     pawns   23
   The king defends against passed pawns by counter-
     attack or blockade   27
2 **When to exchange pieces**   29
   Exchanging while keeping the defender under pressure 29
   Mistimed exchanges   31
   Exchanging when material is level   32
3 **Pawns into queens**   36
   The opposition   38
4 **Winning and drawing techniques**   47
   Queen versus pawn on the seventh rank   47
   Bishop and RP of the wrong colour   49
   Bad bishop handicapped by its own pawns   50
   Stalemate traps   54

PART TWO

ENDGAMES FOR TOURNAMENT
AND MATCH PLAYERS

5 **Rook endgames**   57
   Active rook versus passive rook   58
   The active king   61
   Pawn races   62
   The Philidor and Lucena positions   63
   Tactical decisions   64
   Rook against minor piece   66

6 Textbook theory   68
Advanced techniques in pawn endgames   68
Knight endgames   71
Bishop endgames   74
   Bishops of opposite colours   76
Endgames of bishop against knight without rooks   78
Queen endgames   81
7 Fischer's endgame   86
Anatoly Karpov   93
8 Petrosian's endgame   97
Active versus passive knight   106
9 Adjudication techniques   109
10 Endgame openings   115
Ruy Lopez—Exchange variation   115
Queen's Gambit Declined—Exchange variation   120
French Defence—Tarrasch variation   121
King's Indian Defence—Sämisch variation   124
English Opening   125
Sicilian Defence   126

INTRODUCTION

'Can you advise us what we must do if we want to improve?'
'I don't know what you do at the moment!'
'We study openings a lot, we play a lot, I suppose.'
'But endgames not very much? Do the opposite—study endgames!'

Anatoly Karpov's words above came in reply to an interview question following a simultaneous display at the London Central YMCA Chess Club. Karpov had just shared first prize at Hastings, and he went on to become the leading young contender for Bobby Fischer's world title. It is nothing new for a foreign master to diagnose the endgame as a major weakness of British chess, and the same is true of average club chess in most countries. Many practical players who read this book will have less experience with endings than with other aspects of chess strategy and tactics.

Sessions of four hours or shorter in club and league matches mean that most team games are broken off at an earlier stage than happens in any other major chess nation. Many games go to the adjudicator just when the ending is under way, sometimes even in a stodged up middle game with interlocked pawn chains. Allied to this is the fact that the majority of players simply do not 'like' endings, and prefer to allocate their chess study time to opening variations, traps, and going through newspaper column games (which for space reasons often do not reach an ending).

Adjudications are a fact of chess life, and so are players' personal preferences and dislikes. Most endgame books, as well as general instruction works with an endgame section, concentrate on providing reference material on standard endings. In the conditions of club, match, and even tournament play, it is little surprise that otherwise keen readers study this material with only half-hearted enthusiasm.

If you happen to play a game which is heading towards the standard Lucena position in a rook endgame (Diag. 97) or towards the ending of queen and pawn against queen (Diag. 135) it is odds-on that you won't actually have to win it. In most cases, the position will go for adjudication, the adjudicator will consult a standard reference book such as R. Fine's *Basic Chess Endings* or D. V. Hooper's *A Pocket Guide to Endgames* and you are only involved in work if the adjudicator misreads his text and an appeal is required against his decision.

The result is that it is possible to become quite a strong player with poor endgame technique. The first time I ever had to win the Lucena position was in the 1953 British Championship against C. H. O'D. Alexander, after I had already played for England in the world team championships. My 'technique' in this routine win was so weak that I had to adjourn so as to look up the position in *Basic Chess Endings*.

Many players are less lucky, and the first standard rook and pawn endings they have in tournaments are bungled. So you need to know the Lucena position, and how to win or draw in routine situations like a rook ending with an outside passed pawn (Diag. 101), king and pawn against king (Diag. 42), and bishop and rook pawn of the wrong colour (Diag. 73-75).

Part One of the book, the first four chapters, deals with basic endgame ideas which you should know even if your chess is played only against average opponents. The second part, Chapters 5-10, discusses more advanced techniques which will enable you to score points and half points in tournaments, matches, and postal games against strong opponents from any level from district players to international masters.

But the basic argument of this book is that the amount of routine endgame material you need to learn is limited. To know all the niceties of when rook and pawn against rook is a win and when it is drawn is of little practical value; by the time you reach such a position you will either have forgotten the analysis or else there will be time to look it up during an adjournment.

The types of endgames which will really repay practical study are those which you can aim for right from the opening (this applies to many bishop versus knight situations) rather than those which essentially occur as the result of chance features in the position (as in most queen endings or pawn endings and some rook endings).

Hence, three chapters of this book are particularly important if you want to follow Karpov's good advice and 'study endgames' from a practical viewpoint. One is Chapter 10 on Endgame Openings— situations where a player deliberately steers for a particular endgame right from his choice of opening. The Exchange Variation of the Ruy Lopez, as revived by Fischer, is a good example. In one major variation, White is already on move 4 thinking of a favourable rook and pawn ending. Black can also go for this ending if he thinks the current judgement is incorrect.

Another good endgame opening is the Exchange Variation of the Queen's Gambit. Right from the moment he exchanges pawns in the centre, White has in mind possibilities of achieving a 'minority attack' on the queen's side where his two pawns advance and weaken Black's trio. When the Exchange Variation first appeared in master practice, Black was often caught out by White's strategy and had to struggle in a long defensive endgame, handicapped by a weak QBP—see the game Evans-Opsahl (Diag. 189).

The technique of the endgame opening has been refined further in recent years, and has had spectacular success even at world champion-ship level. The basic theory is that a bishop versus knight ending (with or without rooks on the board) offers very good practical winning chances to the player with the bishop when the pawn chain is flexible and the board is open; while the knight has excellent prospects of scoring when there are fixed and rigid pawn fronts.

Chapter 7 (Fischer's Endgame) and Chaper 8 (Petrosian's Endgame) illustrate the successes of two world champions with this bishop versus knight situation. Fischer has generally preferred to aim for the active bishop, while Petrosian, the master of restraint chess, has opted more often for positions where his opponent's bishop is blocked by a pawn wall and the Petrosian knight can exercise its freedom to manoeuvre.

It is quite possible to aim for either type of endgame according to the position; but in practice many players, like Fischer or Petrosian, will have a preference for one or other minor piece. The consistent successes of the two world champions with these endings have one factor in common. Fischer's endgame and Petrosian's endgame give good winning chances, and the risk of a loss through miscalculation or misjudgment is smaller than in an average middle game position.

They are also practical endings in that a player in a league match who, after 30 or 36 moves, sends up an ending with a knight against a bad bishop and no counterplay for the opponent has fair chances of getting a win on adjudication, even if the situation has not yet progressed to the stage of winning material. Besides this, it is often possible to play endings rapidly and to get in more moves than the minimum allowed for in the playing session.

The endgame opening, Fischer's endgame, and Petrosian's endgame are techniques which master players in the tournaments of the 1970s have assimilated and have at their finger-tips—even if they don't play them quite so well as the world champions. Readers of this book who are accustomed to gear their chess studies mainly to openings will find the ideas of these three chapters easy to grasp—and there are many more opportunities to put the strategies into practice than to win from the Lucena position.

The emphasis in this book is on the ending in relationship to earlier stages of the game, for this is increasingly how it is viewed in master chess. But another aspect of endgame skill is simply to be alert for accidental tactical opportunities, which occur especially in pawn pro-motion situations. Such tactical chances are easily overlooked, as shown by the examples in Chapter 3 of missed opportunities.

So this book should be related to the personal chess experience of its readers. Some will play postal games or major tournament chess, or perhaps social chess, where adjudication is rare—for them the basic positions will be useful. At the other end of the spectrum will be readers who play mainly in inter-club games with adjudication after a mere 30 moves, and who may well have considered till now that endgames were irrelevant in their chess. I hope they too will find the book useful—but whatever kind of chess you play, judge the pages that follow by whether they help you win more games from now on.

The reader is urged to set up each of the examples on his board and play through the moves for himself. Only in this way will he realise the full instructional value of the positions.

Many examples allow of alternative defences not annotated in the text, and the reader will learn much from exploring these and discovering why they do not work. Also many of the games are deliberately left incomplete so that the reader can have the benefit of working out the finishes for himself.

I should like to thank Mr. W. T. McLeod and Mr. R. Mongredien of the publishers, William Collins Sons & Co Ltd, for their very helpful understanding of an author's problems, and Kevin J. O'Connell who suggested many useful examples, particularly in the chapters on the Fischer and Petrosian endgames.

PART ONE

BASIC ENDGAME TECHNIQUE

1

THE KING IN ACTION

A fundamental principle of endgame play is to use your king actively. In the endgame the king is rarely in danger from the opponent's few remaining pieces and can usually be employed aggressively to attack the enemy pawns.

Inexperienced players often keep a king on the back rank in the endgame. Their fear is a snap mate, but it is usually unjustified. In fact, the failure to combine the king with other pieces in the ending is one of the basic weaknesses of endgame play in club chess. Diagram 1 is a random, but typical, example.

1. Barden *v* A. N. Other
(simultaneous, 1971)
White to play

Play continued:

1 B—B5   P—K3?

The first, and already serious mistake. The position, with level material, is an easy draw if Black keeps calm and uses his king actively by 1...K—B2.

2 K—N2   P—R4?

Also weak, since it opens up the black squares for an active invasion by the white king. 2...P—R3 would still probably draw.

3 K—R3   P—K4
4 K—R4   R—K3?

Black's last good chance was 4...N—R2, keeping the white king out.

5 K—N5   N—R2 ch
6 K—R6

2. *Black to play*

Compare the position in Diagram 2 with Diagram 1, a mere six moves earlier. While the black king has remained passive, White's king has marched up the board. White had nothing to fear from mating threats, and now his own king joins with the rook and bishop in direct threats. Black has to do something about 7 R—R8 ch, K—B2; 8 K×N.

6 ...   P—N4 dis ch
7 K×RP   R—QB3
8 B—K7   R—B7
9 K—N6   N—B1 ch
10 K×BP   Resigns

Black's kingless counterplay cannot

15

even get started, because 10. . .R×P loses the knight to 11 R—R8, while otherwise White's active king eats up the remaining black pawns.

An active king can be an advantage in more ways than one. The diagrams in this chapter show how an active king can (*a*) shepherd home passed pawns, (*b*) join in an attack against the enemy king in more complex situations than in diagrams 1 and 2, (*c*) penetrate the enemy position and capture pawns, (*d*) defend against enemy passed pawns by counter-attack or blockade.

The king shepherds home passed pawns

'Passed pawns must be pushed' is a well-worn but slightly misleading piece of endgame lore. The successful advance of a passed pawn normally requires support, and the king is an ideal helper. It can operate aggressively against a solitary enemy defender, and is specially effective when a rook, knight, or bishop is the defending piece trying to blockade the pawn. Then the king's ability to attack a rook or knight from a diagonal, or a bishop via the rank, can force the blockader to retreat and set the passed pawn free to advance further.

Take a look at Diagram 3.

3. Szabo *v* Barcza (*Budapest*, 1955)
White to play

White can march his king up the board to help the QNP to queen. The winning idea goes:

1 P—N6!	P—R5
2 Q—QB8 ch	K—R2
3 P—N7	Q × QP ch
4 K—K1	Q—N5 ch
5 K—Q1	Q—N8 ch
6 K—Q2	Q—N5 ch
7 K—B2	Q—R5 ch
8 K—B3	Q—R4 ch

9 K—B4	Q—Q4 ch
10 K—N4	

Now White's king escapes any perpetual check simply by heading for the new cover provided by the pawn on N7, and then the pawn will be able to queen. But even a world grandmaster like Szabo can underestimate the strength of an active king! In the game White overlooked, or miscalculated, the possible king march, played the weaker 1 Q—K5, and only drew.

The position in Diagram 4 is more complex, but the principle is the same as in Diagram 3. White stands clearly better because his king has already moved to the centre, while Black's king is stranded in the corner. Play continued:

1 P—B4	R—KN3
2 P—Q5	P—KR4
3 P—Q6	N—K3
4 K × P	K—R2
5 P—N4	

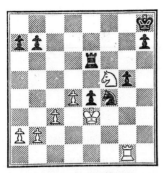

4. Duckstein *v* Kolarov
(*Wageningen*, 1957)
White to play

Played to help support a pawn break at QB6.

5 . . .	P—R5
6 P—B5	P—R4
7 P—R3	P×P
8 P×P	P—R6
9 K—K5	N—Q1
10 P—N5	P—N5
11 P—Q7	

This spoils everything – he should have played 11 N—N3, and only then set about a further king advance.

5. *Black to play*

11 . . .   P—R7?

Black, in turn, goes wrong. He should have played 11. . .R—N4 to hold up the advance of the white king, and then his own pawns are more dangerous, e.g. 12 R—KR1, K—N3 wins the knight, while 12 K—B6, R×N ch!; 13 K×R, P—R7, gives Black a standard win with his united passed pawns against a rook.

12 R—KR1   P—N6

13 N×P!

This deflects the black rook from his guardian function on the third rank.

13 . . .   R×N

Now the white king is free to advance.

14 R×P ch	K—N2
15 K—Q6	N—B2 ch
16 K—B7	R—N4
17 P—B6	R×P
18 P×P	

The two pawns, both protected by the king, are more than a match for Black's forces.

18 . . .	R—QB4 ch
19 K—N6	R—B8
20 R—QN2	N—K4
21 P—Q8=Q	Resigns

6. Orbaan *v* Lindblom
(*Wageningen*, 1957)
White to play

This time (Diagram 6) both players advance their kings:

1 P—B4

White opens the road to the queen's side for his king to travel.

1 . . .   K—B1

Black also knows the importance of an active king.

2 K—B2	K—K2
3 K—K3	

Gaining a tempo through the attack on the bishop . . .

3 . . .	B—B5
4 K—Q2	K—Q3
5 K—B3	K—B3
6 K—N4	

. . . and White reaches the main battle arena first.

6 . . .	P—B3

The only constructive idea left for Black – to try to engineer a passed pawn of his own.

7 P—R5	B—R3

This was essential as White was threatening to play 8 B—R4 ch, and B—N5, cutting off the black bishop from the pawn's route and winning easily.

8 B—R4 ch	K—Q3
9 B—N5	B—N2

This is the difference. Black retains control of vital squares on the QR file – in particular his QR1.

10 P—R6	B—R1

Now Black's bishop is very passively placed.

11 K—R5	P—K4

So Black makes his break and obtains his own passed pawn, but his king is still a long way from supporting the pawn's march to the queening square.

12 QP×P ch	P×P
13 P×P ch	K×P
14 K—N6	

Meanwhile White's own king begins to menace the black bishop.

14 . . .	P—Q5
15 B—Q3!	

Now the black king will have to make a long detour to make any further forward progress, and that would enable White to attack and win the QP.

15 . . .	K—Q3
16 K—R7	B—B6
17 K—N8	K—B4
18 P—R7	K—N5

7. *White to play*

From Diagram 7 White now found a neat tactical solution:

19 B—K2!	Resigns

Why? Both sides found this variation in adjournment analysis, and Black gave up now because the following play is forced: 19. . .B—N7 (or 19. . .B×B; 20 P—R8=Q); 20 P—R8=Q, B×Q, 21 K×B, K—B6; 22 K—N7, P—Q6; 23 B—B3, so that when White captures the pawn, the black king will be decoyed as far away from the king's-side pawns as possible. 23. . .P—Q7; 24 K—B6, K—B7; 25 K—Q5, P—Q8=Q ch; 26 B× Q ch, K×B; 27 K—K5, K—K7; 28 K—B6, K—B6; 29 K—N7, K—N7; 30 K×RP, K×RP; 31 P—N4! wins easily, thanks to White's more active king: 31. . .K—N6; 32 P—N5, K—N5; 33 K×P.

8. Rubinstein *v* Nimzowitsch
(*Carlsbad*, 1907)
White to play

1 N—B3

Unfortunately for White the immediate advance of the king in Diagram 8 miscarries: 1 K—B1, B—B5 ch; 2 K—K1, B—Q4, and Black either exchanges the remaining pieces, leaving himself with a simple win in the king and pawn ending, or wins another pawn.

1 . . .	B—B5
2 P—B4	K—K2
3 K—B2	K—Q3
4 K—K3	K—B4
5 P—N4	K—N5
6 K—Q4	

White approaches the queen's side too late.

6 . . .	B—N6
7 P—N5	P—R5
8 N—N1	B—K3
9 P—N3	K—N6
10 N—B3	P—R6
11 K—Q3	P—N3
12 K—Q4	K—B7!
13 Resigns	

White has no option but to resign, since the knight is now powerless to halt the march of the QRP.

9. Saidy *v* Fischer
(U.S. Championship, 1963–64)
White to play

In this position (Diagram 9) the strain of trying to draw, to stop Fischer obtaining an unprecedented 11–0 score, finally tells on White.

1 B—K1?

Saidy could have kept Fischer's score at 10½–½ by using his king for active king's-side defence: 1 K—K2!, N×P; 2 B—N1, K—B4; 3 K—B3, N—B3; 4 B—R2, N—R4; 5 P—R5!, K—N4; 6 P—KN4, P×P e.p.; 7 B×P, with draw – Black's king can make no progress.

In the game, Fischer's king is able to make a triumphant march: 1...N×P; 2 B—Q2, K—B4; 3 B—K1, N—B3; 4 B—R4, N—K5; 5 B—K1, K—N5; 6 K—K2, N—N6 ch; 7 K—Q3, N—B4; 8 B—B2, N—R5; 9 P—R5, N×P; 10 K—B3, K—B6; 11 B—N1, K—K7; 12 B—R2, P—B6; 13 B—N3, N—K6; 14 Resigns.

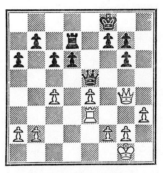

10. Schlechter *v* Lasker
(5th match game, 1910)
Black to play

It is not readily apparent what the position in Diagram 10 has to do with the endgame, but it shows how a World Champion thinks about the endgame *before* it arises.

1 . . .   K—K1

This move is partly made on the general principle of centralization; pieces are generally more effective the nearer they are to the middle of the board. Also, the king can obviously achieve nothing on the king's side, even in the ending. But Lasker also has a long-term vision. He perceives a potential queen's-side passed pawn, and makes ready well in advance to have his king available to shepherd it home.

The game continued: **2 Q—K2, K—Q1; 3 Q—Q2, K—B2; 4 P—R3, R—K2; 5 P—QN4, P—QN4; 6 P × P, RP × P; 7 P—N3, P—N4; 8 K—N2, R—K1; 9 Q—Q1, P—B3; 10 Q—N3, Q—K3; 11 Q—Q1, R—KR1; 12 P—N4, Q—B5.** Black now has a clear advantage. His queen is aggressively posted and cannot be exchanged off *because of the position of the black king*, which, in conjunction with the queen's-side pawns, would be decisive in a queenless ending.

This is an important example of how to think about the endgame – but even World Champions can intersperse far-sighted strategic vision with simple human error. Later in the game, Lasker blundered and lost.

The king joins in an attack against the enemy king

Diagrams 1 and 2 at the start of this chapter show the basic idea of marching a king up the board as far as the sixth rank, so as to join in a mating attack against an opposing king stranded on the back rank. Diagrams 11 to 16 show this theme in more advanced situations from master play.

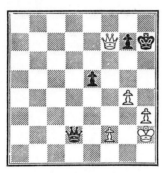

11. Averbakh *v* Suetin
(U.S.S.R. Championship, 1954)
White to play

Averbakh is one of the world's greatest experts on the endgame and immediately perceives, in Diagram 11, the possibility of using his king in a mating attack.

1 K—N3	Q—B6 ch
2 K—R4	Q—Q5
3 Q—B5 ch	P—N3

If the black king retreats to N1 or R1, the result comes just as swiftly. White shifts his king to R5, then carries out the pawn advance P—N5—N6, creating

mating threats; after a check by the black queen on K7 White can play P—B3, and there are no more checks.

4 Q—B7 ch	K—R1
5 Q—B6 ch	K—R2
6 K—N5	Q—Q7 ch
7 P—B4!	P × P

First a black pawn prevents the diagonal check.

| 8 Q—B7 ch | K—R1 |
| 9 K—R6 | Resigns |

If 9. . .P—B6 ch; 10 P—N5 (now it is a white pawn that prevents the check on the diagonal), and mate cannot be prevented.

In Diagram 12 Alekhine has already advanced his king ready for the ending (compare this with the Schlechter *v* Lasker example, Diagram 10), and now the king is able to join a neat attacking combination:

| 1 N—B6 | R(N1)—KB1 |
| 2 R × P | R × N |

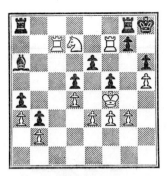

12. Alekhine *v* Yates
(*London*, 1922)
White to play

3 K—K5   Resigns

White wins the exchange. The rook's retreat, or its protection from KB1, is prevented under pain of mate by R—KR7 ch and R(B7)—KN7.

occupy this square to prevent the black pawn queening.

| 3 . . . | K—N4 |
| 4 K—R3 | |

4 B—B7 might prolong White's resistance a little longer.

4 . . .	B—B5
5 Q×P	Q—R8 ch
6 Resigns	

The king invasion has cracked White's resistance. If 6 Q—R2, then 6. . .Q× Q ch; 7 K×Q (hoping for 7. . .B×B ch; 8 K×B, and White has the opposition), 7. . .K—N5, forcing 8 B×B, K×B, and White's king is powerless to stop his black counterpart from having a meal of pawns.

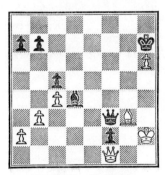

13. Alster *v* Stahlberg
(*Wageningen*, 1957)
White to play

White cannot prevent Black's king from marching up the board in Diagram 13, because White's own counter-chances are restrained by the powerful black pawn at KB7.

1 Q—QN1 ch	K×P
2 Q—QB1 ch	B—K6
3 Q—B1	

Unless giving check, the queen must

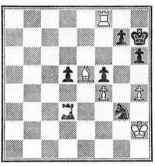

14. Marshall *v* Tarrasch
(5th match game, 1905)
Black to play

In diagram 14 Black is two pawns ahead, but he has a difficult job to advance his QP any further, while an attempt to advance on the other flank would expose Black's own king. So Tarrasch plays for mate:

1 . . .	K—N3
2 R—Q8	N—K5!
3 P—R5 ch	

Or 3 R—Q7, K—R4; 4 R×NP, K×P, and Black is still making progress.

| 3 . . . | K×P |

4	B×P	K—N5
5	R—KN8	R—R6 ch
6	K—N2	R—N6 ch
7	K—B1	

7 K—R1, K—R6, and 8...N—B7 mate, would be just as hopeless.

| 7 | ... | K—B6 |
| 8 | K—K1 | R—N8 mate |

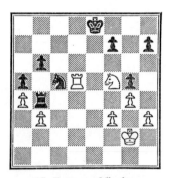

15. Eretova *v* Nicolau
(Women's Olympiad, *Skopje*, 1972)
White to play

Black is about to win the QNP (see Diagram 15), after which the white QRP will also be lost in a few moves. White, in order to obtain some counterplay, has to allow the advance of the black king:

1	N—Q6 ch	K—K2
2	N—B8 ch	K—K3
3	R×P	N×NP
4	R—R5	P—N4!

Seizing the opportunity to create a passed pawn as quickly as possible. If 5 R×NP, R×R; 6 P×R, P—R5, and the white knight cannot get back in time to stop the RP, while if 7 P—N6, then 7...N—B4, followed by the advance of the QRP wins easily.

5	R—R6 ch	K—K4
6	P×P	P—R5
7	R—R6	N—B4
8	R—R5	K—B5

The creation of a passed QRP has lured White's pieces into a corner to prevent its advance. Meanwhile Black can start a king's-side attack, thanks to her active king. See Diagram 16.

16. *White to play*

9	P—N6	R—N7 ch
10	K—B1	K×BP
11	K—N1	K—N6
12	K—B1	N—K5
13	R×P	

This loses the rook, but if 13 K—K1, there follows 13...K—B6; 14 K—Q1, N—B7 ch; 15 K—B1, N—Q6 ch; 16 K—Q1, K—K6, and mate follows.

| 13 | ... | R—N8 ch |
| 14 | Resigns | |

After 14 K—K2, N—B6 ch picks up the rook.

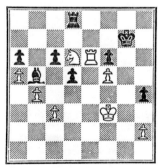

17. Gligoric *v* Stahlberg
(3rd match game, 1949)
White to play

In diagram 17 White is clearly better –

his pieces are more active – but the decisive factor is the ability of his king to penetrate to the heart of the black position. Some care is needed, e.g. 1 N—K8 ch, K—B2; 2 N×P would allow Black to free his position with 2. . . P—Q5!, while 1 N×B, BP×N; 2 R× RP, enables Black to create active play by 2. . .R—QB1.

| 1 K—K3 ! | B—R5 |

White was really threatening 2 N×B: 2. . .BP×N; 3 R×RP, R—QB1; 4 K—Q3. Black prevents this, but now the white king prepares to invade via the dark squares.

| 2 K—Q4 | R—KN1 |

If Black were to sit and do nothing, White's king would force the gain of Black's queen's-side pawns, but in activating his rook, Black's king's field will be exposed to the might of the white rook and knight.

3 K—B5	K—R2
4 N—K8 !	R—N7
5 N×P ch	K—N2
6 N—Q7 !	

Now White's KBP cannot be stopped, directly due to the influence of the white king.

6 . . .	R—KB7
7 P—B6 ch	K—N3
8 N—K5 ch	K—R4

Or 8. . .K—B4; 9 K—Q6.

| 9 P—B7 | P—Q5 |
| 10 R—K8 | Resigns |

The king penetrates the enemy position and captures pawns

Sometimes a king advance, while the enemy king is stranded at the edge, can win material. Often, as in the first examples, Diagrams 1 and 2, this is combined with mating threats. Look now at the position in Diagram 18.

18. From a game at Hastings, 1971
White to play

The white king is able to penetrate:

| 1 K—N4 | K—K3 |
| 2 K—R3 ! | |

Not immediately 2 K×P?, which would be a bad mistake because of 2 . . . K—B4; 3 K—N3, P—N4; 4 P×P K×NP, and Black escapes with a draw

| 2 . . . | Resigns |

Black has no defence. If 2. . .K—B4; 3 K×P, K×P; 4 P—K6 wins, or if 2. . .P—N4; 3 P×P, K×P; 4 K×P, K—B4; 5 K—R5, and wins.

White's king can immediately begin its journey up the board, and with gain of tempo (see Diagram 19).

1 K—B2	B—N2
2 K—N3	K—N2
3 K—B4	K—B2
4 K—K5	K—K2
5 N—Q5 ch	K—B2

19. Fischer *v* Mednis
(U.S. Open Championship, 1957)
White to play

6 K—Q6	B—B1
7 N—B4	B—N5
8 K—B7	B—B6
9 P—B3	

Just in case it should be necessary to put all White's pawns on dark squares, and to create a passed pawn.

9 ...	P—N4
10 P—Q4	P×P
11 P×P	P—N5
12 P—Q5	B×P
13 N×B	K—K3
14 N—B4 ch	K—B4

See Diagram 20. So far, White's king has captured not a single pawn, but its journey has brought with it – by the *threat* to capture the queen's-side pawns – a fatal deterioration in Black's position. After his last move Black thought he was holding the game, for if the knight moves, Black will be able to step round and take the white KRP, but he receives an unpleasant shock . . .

20. *White to play*

15 N×NP!	K×N
16 P—N3	K—B4
17 K—N7	K—N5
18 P—N6	K×P
19 P—N7	Resigns

White's king never did capture even a single pawn, but nevertheless its advance, aimed at winning material, proved decisive.

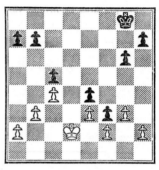

21. Barcza *v* Monostori
(Hungarian Championship, 1951)
White to play

1 P—QN4??

A blunder, throwing away the win he had with 1 K—B3, K—B2; 2 P—QN4, and the white king will be able to penetrate whether or not Black himself exchanges. Similarly 1...P—QR4, to prevent P—QN4, allows K—B3—N2—R3—R4 – a decisive penetration.

1 ...	P×P
2 K—B2	K—B2?

2...P—QR4! would have saved the game for Black: 3 K—N3, P—N3; 4 K—R4, K—B2; 5 K—N5, K—K3; 6 P—B5, P×P; 7 K×BP, K—K4; 8 K—B4, K—Q3; 9 K—Q4, P—R5; 10 K—B4, P—N6; 11 P×P, P—R6; 12 K—B3, K—B4; 13 P—N4 ch, K—N5; 14 K—N3, P—R7; 15 K×P, K×P; 16 K—N2, and White can only draw. As so often in pawn endgames, a single tempo spells the difference between a win and a draw.

3 K—N3	

Now everything is 'normal' again.

3 ...	**K—K3**
4 K×P	**K—Q3**
5 K—N5	**P—N4**
6 P—N4	**P—R3**
7 P—KR3	**P—N3**
8 P—QR4	**K—B2**
9 P—B5	**Resigns**

The finish could be 9...K—N2; 10
P×P, P×P; 11 P—R5!, P×P; 12 K×P,
K—B3; 13 K—N4, and the white king
cannot be prevented from reaching Q4
and then capturing the black pawns at
K4 and B3.

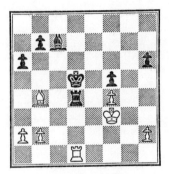

22. Aronin *v* Lutikov
(*Moscow*, 1959)
White to play

Black's king is already well placed in
Diagram 22, and White must now
exchange rooks, so bringing the black
king even further into the heart of his
position.

1 R×R ch	

If 1 R—QB1, then 1...R×B; 2 R×B,
R×NP.

1 ...	**K×R**
2 B—B3 ch	

White's own king cannot prevent the
black king's infiltration, because it is
tied to the defence of the pawn at KB4.

2 ...	**K—Q6**
3 B—N7	**P—KR4**
4 B—K5	**B—R4**

The exchange is clearly impossible, as
Black's king could not catch the KP.

5 B—B6	**P—N4**
6 B—N7	**B—Q7**

Black does not need to rush, and so
he steadily strengthens his position by
centralizing his pieces.

7 B—B6	**B—B8**
8 B—K5	**K—B7**

The final mopping-up begins.

23. *White to play*

9 P—N3	**K—N8**
10 K—N3	

Or 10 P—QR4, P—N5!

10 ...	**K×P**
11 K—R4	

White's king can also get amongst the
pawns, but it is too late. The game
concluded: **11**...K×P; **12** K×P, K—
B5; **13** K—N6, P—N5; **14** P—R4, K—
N6; **15** P—R5, P—N7; **16** P—R6, P—
N8=Q; **17** P—R7, Q—N3 ch; **18** K—
N5. Or 18 K—R5, Q—Q1; 19 P—R8=
Q, Q×Q ch; 20 B×Q, B×P; 21 K—
N6, B—Q7; 22 K×P, B—B6!, forcing
the exchange of bishops with an easy
win. **18**...Q—Q1 ch; **19** K—N6, Q—
K1 ch; **20** K—N5, Q×B!; **21** Resigns.

In Diagram 24 Botvinnik has an extra
pawn, but it is clearly difficult for him
to create a passed pawn, so a king
march is in order:

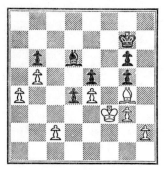

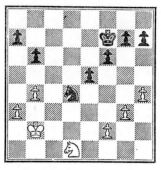

24. Botvinnik *v* Pachman
(Leipzig, 1960)
White to play

1 K—K2	B—N5
2 K—Q3	K—B3
3 K—B4	B—K8
4 K—Q5	B—N5?

This allows White's bishop to penetrate to K8 without difficulty, whence it ties the black king to the defence of the rear KNP. Black could have made White's task more difficult with 4...B—B6, to answer 5 B—Q7 with 5...K—K2.

| 5 B—Q7 | B—K8 |

If 5...K—K2, White wins by the sacrifice 6 K×KP, K×B; 7 K—B6.

| 6 B—K8 | B—B6 |
| 7 K—B6 | Resigns |

Black, a world-class player himself, saw that if 7...B—R4; 8 K—B7, K—N2; 9 K—Q6, K—B3; 10 B×P!, K× B; 11 K×P, B—B6; 12 K—K6, P—N5; 13 P—K5, B—N5; 14 K—Q7, K—B2; 15 P—K6 ch, K—B1; 16 P—R5 wins. Black's bishop cannot face both ways at once.

———————————————

Black's extra pawn (Diagram 25) gives him an easy win, but this is achieved with beautiful clarity and logic:

1 ...	K—K3
2 K—B3	N—N4 ch
3 K—N3	K—Q4

25. Marshall *v* Tarrasch
(Ostend, 1905)
Black to play

The black king cannot be prevented from carrying out a decisive infiltration on the light squares.

4 P—R4	N—Q5 ch
5 K—B3	K—K5
6 P—N5	

If 6 K—Q2, then 6...K—B6; 7 K—Q3, P—KR4!, and 8...P—KN4! wins easily.

| 6 ... | K—B6 |
| 7 K—Q3 | N—K3 |

Beginning an eleven-move combination to force a neat win.

8 K—B4	K—K7
9 N—B3 ch	K×P
10 K—Q5	N—B4
11 P—QR5	P—K5

Black's king has prepared the way for this advance, which should now be carried out as rapidly as possible.

12 P×P	P×P
13 K—B6	P—K6
14 K×P	N—R5 ch!

The point of the combination. White's knight is distracted from its role as bulwark against the advance of the KP.

| 15 N×N | P—K7 |
| 16 N—B5 | |

16 N—N2, to answer 16...P—K8= Q? with 17 N—Q3 ch, would also be met by 16...K—K6.

16 . . .	K—K6
17 K—R7	

Resignation was called for. The finish was: **17...P—K8=Q; 18 P—N6, Q×P; 19 P—N7, P—B4; 20 N—K6, Q×**

P!; 21 P—N8=Q, Q—R5 ch; 22 K—N6, Q—N6 ch; 23 K—B7, Q×Q ch; 24 K×Q, P—B5; 25 N×NP, P—B6; 26 N—R5, P—B7; 27 N—N3, P—R4; 28 K—B7, P—R5; 29 N—B5 ch, K—B5; 30 Resigns.

The king defends against passed pawns by counter-attack or blockade

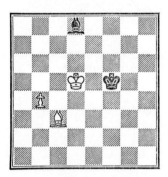

26. *Black to play*

Janowski (Black) resigned in this position (Diagram 26) against Capablanca in New York, 1916. He could, however, have drawn by using his king to inaugurate a counter-attack against White's passed QNP: **1...K—B5; 2 B—Q4, K—B6; 3 P—N5, K—K7; 4 K—B6, K—Q6; 5 B—N6, B—R5; 6 K—N7, K—B5; 7 K—R6, K—N6; 8 B—K3, B—Q1; 9 B—Q2, K—R5,** and the pawn can make no progress without immediately being hacked off by Black's bishop.

White cannot save his QRP, but by counter-attacking on the king's side he can put up a satisfactory defence, see Diagram 27:

1 K—K4	K×P
2 P—B5!	P×P ch

White threatened 3 P×P, P×P; 4 P—R5.

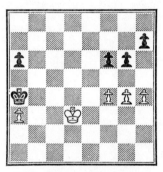

27. Van Doesburgh *v* Maroczy
(*Zandvoort*, 1936)
White to play

3 K×P	P—QR4
4 K×P	P—R5
5 K—N7!	

Not 5 P—N5?, K—N5; 6 P—R5, P—R6; 7 P—N6, P×P; 8 P×P, P—R7; 9 P—N7, P—R8=Q ch, and wins.

5 . . .	K—N5
6 K×P	P—R6
7 P—N5	P—R7
8 P—N6	P—R8=Q
9 P—N7	

A theoretical draw (see Chapter 4, Diagram 71), but grandmaster Maroczy hopes to bamboozle his less experienced opponent. The further course of the game was: **9...Q—R2; 10 K—R8, Q—Q5; 11 P—R5, Q—B3; 12 K—R7, Q—B4 ch; 13 K—R6!, Q—B3 ch. Or 13...Q—B2; 14 P—N8=Q!, Q×Q stalemate. 14 K—R7, Q—B4 ch; 15 K—R6, Q—K3 ch; 16 K—R7, Q—B2; 17 P—R6,**

K—B4; **18 K—R8, Q—KN3.** If 18. . .
Q—KB3, not 19 P—R7??, Q—K4 and
mates!, but simply 19 K—R7. **19 P—
N8=Q, Q×P ch; 20 Q—R7, Q×Q ch;
21 K×Q. Draw agreed.**

From Diagram 28 it is a case of a
blockade draw achieved at a single
stroke. White played **1 K—B2!** and
Black immediately conceded half a
point The white king can never be
shifted from KB2 as long as the white
knight controls KN3, and so stops
Black playing . . .P—N6 ch. Black can
manoeuvre his bishop to KN7 to take
away the knight's squares at KB1 and
KR1, but then the agile knight can

28. Belyavsky *v* Kuzmin
(U.S.S.R. Championship, 1973)
White to play

equally well commute from KN3 to
KB5 or KR5. So, a **draw.**

2
WHEN TO EXCHANGE PIECES

Cashing in on a material advantage – what masters call technique – and knowing the right time to exchange pieces, are key factors in successful winning endgame play. In many endgames where you are a pawn or the exchange up, the basic approach is to keep your opponent under pressure while seizing chances gradually to reduce the pieces on the board. Every simplification, without disadvantage to your own position, means that the relative value of your own material superiority is greater.

All masters are accurate in these situations. The chief error made by amateur players is to exchange prematurely, to go into an even simpler ending without first strengthening the position. Psychologically speaking, such mistakes are caused by instinctive and natural caution, and they are seen from a very early stage of players' chess experience. Recently I witnessed an extreme example in an inter-area junior school's team match, where a girl had a queen and knight against her boy opponent's rook. She thought for a little, her eyes lit up, and she exchanged off all the pieces into what she clearly anticipated would be a winning king and pawn endgame. Alas, it proved to be drawn. This type of mistake, in more sophisticated form, occurs frequently in club chess.

This chapter looks at three aspects of exchanging. In the first section, one side has a material advantage and exchanges correctly, keeping the defender under pressure; second, one side has a material advantage but mistimes his exchanges at the cost of positional disadvantage; and third, we examine exchanging technique in situations where material is level.

Exchanging while keeping the defender under pressure

Let us now look at some examples of how a grandmaster, facing strong opposition, uses his material advantage in an active way by keeping the opponent tied down to a passive position and, at the same time, taking his chances to simplify.

29. Petrosian *v* Karpov
(U.S.S.R. Championship, 1973)
White to play

In Diagram 29 Petrosian's first objective is to strengthen his position.

1 N—N5	B—K2
2 P—KR4	K—K3
3 N—Q4 ch	K—Q2
4 K—N2	B—B3
5 N—N5	B—K2
6 P—R4	P—R3
7 P—R5!	

Notice the value of this move, the effect of which is to weaken Karpov's KBP, so that Black's previously compact pawn formation of two 'islands' (inter-supporting groups) is changed into a weak group of three islands, which can be attacked by the white knight.

7 . . .	P × P
8 B—B2	B—Q1
9 N—Q4	P—B5
10 N—K2	K—B3
11 N × P	

. . . first the KBP and then the KRP (move 17).

11 . . .	P—R5
12 N—N6	N—N2
13 P—B4	B—B3
14 R—B1 ch	N—B4
15 K—R3	N—Q3
16 B × N	

Notice that Petrosian did not immediately (on move 1) exchange off his active knight for Black's passive knight

at Q3. He preferred further strengthening of the position, and now that an exchange of the white bishop for the black knight does come, it is not, as might have been expected, at Black's Q3, where the black knight was pinned, but at QB4. By capturing on this square, Petrosian can force yet another weakness in the black position and make the win quite simple: **16. . .P × B; 17 N × P, P—R4; 18 N—B3, K—Q4; 19 R—Q1 ch, B—Q5; 20 N—Q2, K—K3; 21 K—N3, N—B4 ch; 22 K—B3, P—R5; 23 N—B4, B—B6; 24 K—N4, B—N5; 25 R—Q3, Resigns.**

30. Portisch *v* Forintos
(Hungarian Championship, 1971)
Black to play

| 1 . . . | B—K3 ? |

1. . .B—N1 is correct and should draw. White cannot then make any progress despite his extra material.

1. . .R × R would lose to 2 P × R ch, K—B3; 3 R—QR7, and the passed BP decides.

Black's error in the game gave White the opportunity to exchange into a simply won ending. He played . . .

| 2 R × R ch | K × R |
| 3 R × B ch! | |

and **Black resigned,** because after 3. . . K × R; 4 K—R5, K—B2; 5 K × P, K—N1; 6 K—N6, White's pawn cannot be stopped.

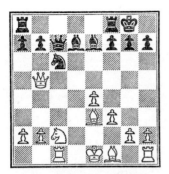

31. Lombardy *v* Fischer
(U.S. Championship, 1960–61)
Black to play

In Diagram 31 White has a material advantage which, given the chance, he might hope to convert into a win in the endgame, but Fischer has seen that he can turn the position into a winning ending for himself.

1 ...	N—N5
2 N×N	Q×R ch
3 B×Q	B×Q
4 N—Q5	B—R5 ch!

Fischer shows his superb technique.

| 5 P—N3 | B×B |
| 6 R×B | |

If 6 P×B, then 6...B—N7 is deadly.

| 6 ... | B—Q1 |

Black now has a material advantage, and proceeds to consolidate ... and to complete his development!

| 7 B—Q2 | R—B1 |
| 8 B—B3 | P—B4! |

Undermining the white knight.

9 P—K5	R—B4
10 N—N4	B—R4
11 P—QR3	B×N
12 P×B	R—Q4
13 K—K2	K—B2
14 P—R4	K—K3

Black has steadily increased his grip and now brings his king into action.

15 K—K3	R—B1
16 R—KN1	R—B5
17 R—K1?	

White could still make things difficult with 17 R—QR1, P—QR3; 18 R—KN1.

32. *Black to play*

Black now has the opportunity for another advantageous exchange of material, see Diagram 32:

| 17 ... | R×B ch! |

Last time it was to reach an ending material up, now the material is returned for a simple win in a king and pawn ending: **18 P×R, R×P ch; 19 K—Q2, R×R; 20 K×R, K—Q4; 21 K—Q2, K—B5; 22 P—R5, P—QN3; 23 K—B2, P—KN4; 24 P—R6, P—B5; 25 P—N4, P—R4; 26 P×P, P×P; 27 K—N2, P—R5; 28 K—R3, K×P; 29 K×P, K—Q5; 30 K—N4, K—K6; 31 Resigns.**

Mistimed exchanges

Now we come on to the situation where one side has a material advantage but fails to evaluate it in the correct way. The most usual failure is to mistime exchanges and to give the opponent chances for counterplay from a previously passive defence. See Diagram 33.

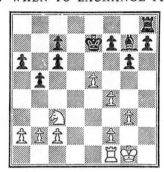

33. Bednarski *v* Smyslov
(Olympiad, *Skopje*, 1972)
White to play

White has several advantages in this ending: he has a good knight against a bad bishop, and a king's-side pawn majority. Black's corresponding majority on the other flank has no real chance of producing a passed pawn, so for practical purposes White is a pawn ahead. The ending should be a matter of technique.

1 K—N2

White immediately starts to go wrong. 1 N—K4, making the most of the powerful knight, was correct, since 1...R—Q1, apparently seizing the queen's file, can always be met by R—K1, followed by K—B1, K—K2, and R—Q1, forcing the black rook away from the open file or else exchanging under favourable circumstances, into a good knight versus bad bishop endgame.

1 ...   **R—Q1**
2 R—Q1?

Now this is wrong. White assumes that once the rooks are exchanged, he has a winning ending, but that is true only if the rooks can be exchanged without having to make important positional concessions. Here the knight is temporarily drawn out of play This may seem a trivial concession, but it is enough for Smyslov to be able to save the game and almost turn the tables! 2 K—B3 was correct, e.g. 2...R—Q7; 3 R—QB1 and 4 K—K3.

2 ...   **R×R**
3 N×R   **K—K3**
4 K—B3   **P—N4!**

Had White not allowed his knight to be decoyed to the back rank, then this move could have been prevented by N—K4.

Black has been given just enough time to break up White's constricting king's-side pawn formation.

5 P×P

White now has to exercise care, e.g. 5 K—K4?, P×P; 6 P×P, P—B4 ch!, and the outside passed pawn gives Black the better ending.

5 ...   **K×P**
6 N—K3   **P—QB4**
7 P—N3   **B—B1**
8 K—K2   **K—Q5**
9 K—Q2   **Draw agreed**

White just hangs on! 9...K—K5; 10 K—K2, K—Q5; 11 K—Q2, leads to a draw by repetition, while 9...P—B5 is too risky, for after 10 P—B3 ch, K—K5; 11 P×P, P×P; 12 K—K2, White has some winning chances.

Exchanging when material is level

The ideas mentioned in the previous two sections apply equally when an endgame advantage is positional rather than material. You should always be alert for decisive simplification manoeuvres and combinations. A good example of this is shown in Diagram 34.

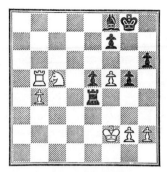

34. Hearst *v* Fischer
(Metropolitan League, 1957)
Black to play

Fischer now played the decisive...

1 ... R×P!

Taking the opportunity to win material, and threatening simply to exchange off pieces into an easily won king and pawn ending.

2 R—R5

2 R×R, B×N ch, and 3...B×R, is even worse for White.

2 ...	B×N ch
3 R×B	R—B5 ch
4 K—K3	R×P

Black has won two pawns and went on to win easily after: 5 P—N4, R—B5; 6 P—R3, P—K5; 7 R—B4, R—B6 ch; 8 K×P, R×P; 9 K—K5, R—K6 ch; 10 K—B6, R—B6 ch; 11 K—K5, K—N2; 12 K—Q5, K—N3; 13 R—B1, R—B5; 14 R—KN1, P—B4; 15 P×P ch, K×P; 16 R—KR1, K—N3; 17 K—K5, P—R4; 18 R—QB1, P—R5; 19 R—KN1, K—R4; 20 R—KR1, R—B1; 21 R—Q1, P—R6; 22 K—K4, K—R5; 23 R—Q7, R—B8; 24 R—Q2, P—N5; 25 R—Q8, P—R7; 26 Resigns.

White, in Diagram 35, has a much superior ending thanks to his better placed pieces and more compact pawn formation, which should be enough to win. White sees the chance to exchange

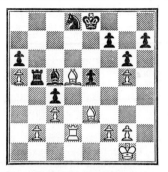

35. Barden *v* Penrose
(British Championship,
Plymouth, 1957)
White to play

off into an ending where he will be a pawn up, and he grabs it:

1 B×QBP	R×RP
2 B×B?	

But this is dubious – the exchange is made at the cost of White's positional advantage. White is in too much of a hurry to capture the QRP, and get into an ending a pawn up, with two connected passed pawns on the queen's side.

The right approach was to keep Black under pressure with 2 R—Q5!, and only then think of exchanges.

2 ...	R×B
3 B×RP	N—K3

White cannot even keep his extra pawn.

4 K—B1	R—R4
5 B—N7	N×P

Now, with his material advantage gone the same way as his positional advantage, White begins to drift into trouble: 6 P—QB4, N—K3; 7 B—B6 ch, K—K2; 8 R—Q7 ch, K—B3; 9 K—K1, R—R3; 10 B—Q5, R—N3; 11 R—N7, R×R; 12 B×R, N—B4; 13 B—B3, P—K5; 14 B—K2, K—K4; 15 K—Q2, K—Q5; 16 P—QN4, N—R3; 17 P—N5, N—B4; 18 K—B2?, P—B4; 19 K—Q2, P—B5; 20 P—N3, P—B6; 21 B—B1, P—R4; 22 B—R3, K×P; 23 P—N6, K—N4; 24 B—K6, P—N4; 25 K—K3,

K×P; 26 B—B5, K—B3; 27 B—N6, K—Q4; 28 B×P, N—Q2; 29 B—N6, N—B3; 30 B—B5, K—K4; 31 P—N4, N—Q4 ch; 32 K—Q2, K—B5; 33 Resigns. So died one player's hopes of winning the 1957 British Championship.

Dickinson v Barden, Bayswater Open, 1971. This game illustrates a common situation in practical tournament chess. The weaker player, in this case White, simply tries to draw by exchanging at every opportunity. This situation often leads, as here, to a semi-endgame with the queens off the board early.

1 P—K4, P—KN3; 2 P—Q4, B—N2; 3 P—QB4, P—Q3; 4 N—QB3, N—KB3; 5 P—B3, P—K4; 6 P×P, P×P; 7 Q×Q ch, K×Q; 8 B—K3, P—B3.

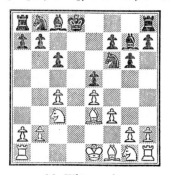

36. *White to play*

The game is equal, except that White has already created holes on his QB5 and Q4 squares.

Black has to improve his position all the time and to look for two opportunities:

(*a*) to get into a winning ending, for example active against passive bishop (this might occur after an exchange of dark-squared bishops at White's K3). and;

(*b*) to win in a more direct way.

9 P—KN4?   K—B2
10 B—Q3   KN—Q2
11 KN—K2   N—R3
12 P—QR3   N(R3)—B4

13 B—QB2   P—QR4

White's strategy has been dubious. His 9 P—KN4, put another pawn on a light square, and so increased his potential bad bishop problem. Meanwhile, Black has activated most of his pieces, and now takes the initiative on the queen's side. His plan is to fix White's pawns by ...P—R5 and/or swap off White's active bishop by ...N—K3 and ...B—B1—QB4.

14 N—R4   N×N
15 B×N   B—B1

The KB also heads for the queen's side, but White has exchanged a pair of knights, and is content to await developments.

16 N—B3   N—B4
17 B—QB2   B—K3
18 P—N3   P—R5!

Black could continue his policy of aiming for a good bishop versus bad bishop ending, as discussed in the note to move 8, but this pawn sacrifice is sharper. If 19 P—N4, the black knight has a safe landing on QN6, and White's QBP is insufficiently protected.

19 B×N   B×B
20 N×P   B—Q5
21 O—O—O

37. *Black to play*

In Diagram 37, White's exposed castled position on the queen's side, his exchanges on that flank, and his capture of Black's sacrificed QRP, have opened up lines which give Black the opportunity to decide the game by a direct attack against the white king. This is a general theme in the early stages of endgames, where the player with the advantage often has the option between aiming for a purely endgame-type advantage (see the note to Black's 18th move) or of exploiting his position by attacking middle game-style methods.

21 . . .	P—QN4
22 P×P	P×P
23 N—N2	R×P

Now White's next move is already desperate. The threats are 24...B×QNP and 24...R—QB1.

24 R×B	P×R
25 R—Q1	R—R8 ch
26 K—Q2	R×R ch
27 N×R	P—R4
28 P—N5	R—R1
29 P—K5	R—R6
30 Resigns	

To conclude this chapter, a repeat on the theme. Before exchanging pieces in an endgame, try to ensure that the initiative is maintained. If your swap entails positional concessions such as giving an active role to some of your opponent's pieces, which were previously confined to defence, then you should try to strengthen your position further before embarking on your exchanging plan.

3

PAWNS INTO QUEENS

The push of a passed pawn through to queen is a theme at the heart of many chess endgames, and it illustrates how one of the key features of successful play is surprise. Surprise in the opening means a prepared repertoire variation, taking your opponent out of his known theory and gaining a permanent initiative or positional advantage as the reward for your pre-game homework. Surprise in the middle game means tactical play and combinative attack, which demonstrates that the opponent's king was less well defended than he thought.

The most important surprise situation in the endgame occurs in the final stages of pushing through to queen against a stubborn defence. There are many situations where a single, far-advanced pawn, or a 3 to 2 or 4-3 pawn majority on either flank, has just enough time to become decisive before the opponent's defensive forces can blockade or surround it. A pawn ahead, which in the opening or middle game may be a marginal or dubious plus, spells in the endgame the difference between a full point and a draw or defeat.

During routine technical endgames, promotion is the last stage of the mopping-up process. When your king has successfully invaded the enemy position, and can shepherd the pawn through to queen, backed by an active against a passive rook, then the win is not difficult. Most endgames belong to this technical group, but alertness to passed pawn tactics can bring you many extra valuable points. A player with a sense for queening combinations can often set them up many moves beforehand.

The schematic examples of promotion occur in the pure pawn endgames. Diagrams 38 and 39 show White sacrificing one or more pawns to create a passed pawn of his own with a free run.

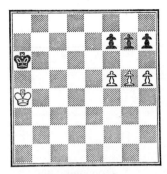

38. *White to play*

With a pawn on the sixth or seventh rank, the tactical possibilities become very frequent. An alert player should be able to spot many of them, even if in general he has a poor eye for sacrifices.

40. *White to play*

In Diagram 38 White clears the road for one of his pawns by **1 P—N6,** and now, if 1...RP×P, then 2 P—B6, P×BP; 3 P—R6, or if 1...BP×P, then 2 P—R6, P×RP; 3 P—B6, and wins.

39. *White to play*

Diagram 39 has a trap for White, which shows how a single routine move in a queening situation can give away a valuable half point. After the obvious 1 P—B4?, P—B3, White can no longer obtain a passed pawn, and the game is a draw.

The correct sequence of moves is **1 P—B6, P×P; 2 P—B4,** followed by **3 P—N5,** and White queens by force. Diagrams 38 and 39 show that queening combinations are in the air in simple positions, once a pawn has got as far as the fifth rank, and the opposing king or other blockading pieces are distant.

Diagram 40 is an endgame which shows the idea of Diagrams 38 and 39 recurring in a slightly more complex form. The two factors which should set White looking for a tactical queening idea are his strong advanced pawn on the sixth rank, with a companion not far behind on the fourth, and the distant black king which handicaps the defence. White won by **1 P—R5, K—B3.** If 1...N×B, then 2 P—R6. **2 B—B8, K—K2; 3 B×P, N×B; 4 P—R6,** and queens. Another facet of the play from Diagram 40 is that the knight is a poor defensive piece against passed pawns. In the final position after 4 P—R6, White would win the game even without his NP.

It is possible to create positions like Diagram 40 once it becomes clear that the game is headed for simplification and exchanges of queens and rooks. Diagram 41, was reached by a stodged up King's Indian Defence opening which seemed to be petering out with multiple exchanges on the open queen's

41. Barden *v* Phillips (1971)
Black to play

file. Ashamed to offer a draw because the same two opponents had been widely criticized for drawing ten games out of twelve in a British Championship play-off match, White hopefully advanced his queen's-side pawns until the spearhead arrived at QN6.

Of course in normal circumstances Black, an international player, would have observed the coming sacrifice and defended by 1...B—B1. But, short of time, he played the routine **1...K—B2?; 2 B×RP!** (2...P×B; 3 P—N7, and the pawn queens) and White's extra pawn was sufficient for a win on adjudication a few moves later.

The Opposition

Diagram 42 shows a standard winning idea in pawn endgames—the opposition. When two kings face each other with a single empty square intervening, whoever has the move must retreat or step aside. The opponent is said to have the opposition, and this factor of forcing an opponent to concede space is a key idea in king and pawn endgames. Zugzwang – roughly translatable as 'movebound' – occurs when a player has only losing moves at his disposal, and the opposition is simply a special form of zugzwang.

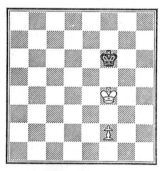

42. *White to play*

With Black to move in Diagram 42, White clearly has the opposition and wins: 1...K—N3; 2 K—K5, K—B2; 3 K—B5, K—N2; 4 K—K6, K—N3; 5 P—B4, and the pawn advances through to queen. If it is White's move, then Black has the opposition, but White has a winning resource: **1 P—B3!**, K—K3; 2 K—N5, K—B2; 3 K—B5. Not 3 P—B4?, K—N2!, when Black has the

opposition and draws, but now after 3 K—B5, White has the opposition and wins. **3...K—N2; 4 K—K6, K—B1; 5 P—B4, K—K1; 6 P—B5, K—B1; 7 K—B6.** Keeping the opposition. Again not 7 P—B6?, K—K1, and draws. **7...K—K1; 8 K—N7,** and White wins. If White's pawn had originally stood on B3 instead of B2, there would be no way for White to gain the opposition, and the game would be drawn.

The technique of opposition and pawn promotion can be tricky, requiring a tactical solution, even in such a simple position as in Diagram 43. **1 P—B7 ch, K—B1,** and now White must not play 2 K—B6, because that is stalemate. **2 K—Q7!.** It may seem surprising that the pawn can be sacrificed, but the sequel shows why. **2...K×P; 3 K—Q6, K—B1; 4 K—K6, K—N2; 5 K—K7, K—R1; 6 K—B6, K—R2; 7 K—B7,**

43. Golombek v Pomar
(*London*, 1946)
White to play

K—R1; 8 K×P, K—N1; 9 K—B6, K—
R2; 10 K—B7, K—R1; 11 K—N6, K—
N1; 12 K—R6, K—R1; 13 P—N6, K—
N1; 14 P—N7. It is very important that
this should not be a check. 14...K—B2;
15 K—R7, Black resigns.
See also Chapter 6.

The next position, Diagram 44, shows
how even a world class grandmaster can
fail to solve the problems of promotion
technique.

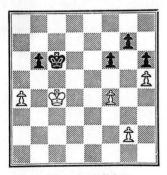

44. Gligoric v Eliskases
(*Mar del Plata*, 1950)
White to play

White can queen a pawn with **1 P—
B5**, which 'fixes' the black pawns.
Gligoric played 1 P—N4, and only drew
after 1. .K—Q3; 2 K—N5, K—B2; 3

K—R6, P—B4; 4 P×P, K—B3; 5 K—
R7, P—QN4; 6 P×P ch, K×P; 7 K—
N7, K—B4; 8 K—B7, K—Q4; 9 K—
Q7, K—K5; 10 K—K6, K×P(B5); 11
P—B6, P×P; 12 K×P, K—K5. White
wins the KRP, but then cannot escape
from the path of his own.
   1...K—B2; 2 K—N5, K—N2; 3 P—
N3, K—B2; 4 K—R6, K—B3; 5 P—N4,
K—B2; 6 K—R7, K—B3; 7 K—N8, P—
QN4; 8 P×P ch, K×P; 9 K—B7, K—
B4; 10 K—Q7, K—Q4; 11 K—K7, K—
K4; 12 K—B7, K—B5; 13 K×P, K—
N4; 14 K—B7, and wins.
   Above all, pawn promotion situations
test your tactical flair and imagination.
To sharpen your alertness for queening,
and other pawn promotion opportunities
cover up the moves after each of the
Diagrams 45–69 and work out for
yourself how White or Black forced a
tactical win.

45. *White to play*

In this study position by O. Duras,
Diagram 45, White's problem is how to
utilize the advantages of his slightly
better king position, and of moving
first, to force the black king to a square
where White's pawn can queen with
check. So **1 K—B5!**, P—N4. If 1...K—
N3, then 2 P—N4, K—B2; 3 P—N5,
K—K2 fails to 4 K—B6!, K—Q1; 5 K—
N7 followed by 6 K—R7, 7 P—N6,
8 P—N7, and 9 P—N8=Q ch. **2 P—
N4**, P—N5; **3 K—Q4** – a typical plan
in pawn races. White utilizes the threat
to blockade the black pawn to force

Black's king to a bad square. **3...K—N4; 4 P—N5, P—N6; 5 K—K3, K—N5; 6 P—N6, K—R6; 7 P—N7, P—N7; 8 K—B2, K—R7; 9 P—N8=Q ch,** wins.

and White wins by advancing his king up the board to help a pawn through (as we saw in Chapter 1).

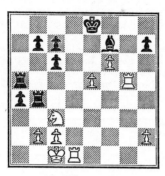

46. *White to play*

The game (see Diagram 46) was played in Odessa 1972. White forced a pawn through to queen with **1 P—K6!, R×R; 2 R—Q8 ch!, K×R; 3 P×B, Black resigns.**

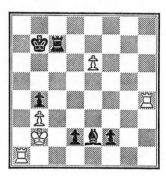

48. *Black to play*

The game (see Diagram 48) was won by the 1973 World Junior Champion, Belyavsky, in 1972. If Black queens either pawn then White gives up the rook on QR1 for it, wins another pawn by R × NP ch, then puts his other rook behind Black's last pawn to force a draw. Belyavsky found a win with **1...R—B7 ch!; 2 K×R, P—Q8=Q ch; 3 R×Q, B×R ch; 4 K×B, P—B8= Q ch,** and White resigns.

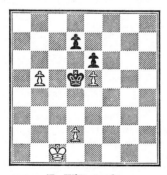

47. *White to play*

In this study position, Diagram 47, White has a neat tactical method of forcing a pawn through. The obvious 1 P—N6, fails against the simple 1... K—B3. So **1 P—Q4, P—Q3; 2 P—N6, K—B3; 3 P—Q5 ch!, K×NP; 4 QP× P, K—B3; 5 P—K7, K—Q2; 6 P×P,**

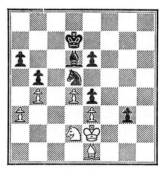

49. Reshevsky *v* Hort ('World 5-minute Championship', *Yugoslavia,* 1970) *Black to play*

50. *White to play*

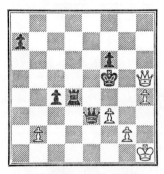

51. Kaufman *v* R. Byrne
(U.S. Championship, 1972)
Black to play

52. Ghitescu *v* Tringov
(Olympiad, *Skopje*, 1972)
White to play

A neat tactic provided a rapid promotion to queen in Diagram 49: **1...P—N7; 2 B—B2. 2 K—B2, B—N6 ch!; 2...N—B6 ch. 2...B—R7,** would probably win also, but is much slower and not as neat. **3 K—K1, B—N6!,** and **Reshevsky resigned,** because the pawn must queen.

In this endgame study, Diagram 50, White has a tactical solution, but he must be very accurate, e.g. he would only draw after 1 P×P, P×P; 2 N× P ch, when Black can sacrifice his bishop for White's last pawn. **1 P—N5 ch!, K—B2; 2 N—Q6!, K×N; 3 K—N7, B—B2; 4 K—B8!.** Now Black has to lose his bishop, and then White captures the black NP and queens his own, e.g. 4... K—B4; 5 K×B, K—N5; 6 K×P, K×P; 7 K—B6, and White easily queens before Black.

Another example of an active king (see Diagram 51): **1...K—B5.** Not 1... K—K3?; 2 Q—K8 ch, and White wins. **2 Q—R6 ch, K—N6; 3 Q×Q, R—Q8 ch; 4 Q—N1, R×Q ch; 5 K×R, P—R4!.** White had overlooked the point that Black need not stop to capture the KRP. **6 P—R5, P—B6; 7 P×P, P—R5,** and White resigned, because of 8 P—R6, P—R6; 9 P—R7, P—R7; 10 P—R8=Q, P—R8=Q mate.

See Diagram 52. **1 P—Q6!, Q—R2 ch.** If 1...Q—K3, then 2 R×R, Q×R (or 2...Q—K8 ch; 3 R—B1 ch); 3 P—Q7 ch, K—K2; 4 Q×Q ch, K×Q; 5 P—Q8=Q. **2 K—N2, P—N7; 3 Q—R8 ch, Black resigns,** because if 3...K—Q2, then 4 R×R ch, K×P; 5 R×Q, P—N8=Q; 6 Q—Q8 ch, and White soon forces mate. This theme of being able to force mate is an extremely important one in pawn promotion situations, where both sides may queen, and in such situations you must look carefully for the existence of mating possibilities.

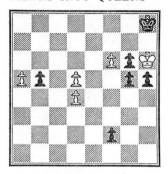

53. *White to play*

White to play and win from Diagram 53 is not a printing error! **1 P—R6, P—B8=Q; 2 P—R7, Q—QR8; 3 P—B7, Q—R6; 4 P—Q6!**, and the black queen cannot stop White queening a pawn and forcing mate.

If it were White's move in Diagram 54, he could mate by 1 R—K7 ch, but it is Black's move, so he just has one tempo which he can use by **1...Q× BP ch!; 2 Q×Q, P×R**, and **White resigns** as there is no defence to 3...P—N8=Q.

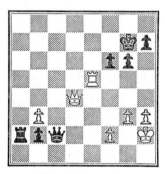

54. *Black to play*

See Diagram 55 **1...R×R; 2 P—B7, P—R7?**. The Yugoslav grandmaster should have played 2...R×P ch!; 3 K×R, K×P, when Black captures the white pawns, and queens his own. **3 P×R=Q, P—R8=Q ch; 4 K—R2, K×P; 5 Q—N5 ch, Black resigns.**

56. *Black to play*

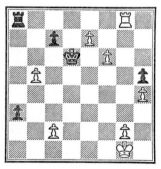

55. Timman *v* Ivkov
(*Amsterdam*, 1971)
Black to play

In Diagram 56 Black can force one of his pawns home by **1...P—K8= Q ch!**. Instead he chose 1...N×P, whereupon White mopped up his opponent's passed pawns by 2 N—K5 ch, K—N2; 3 N×P, followed by 4 K×P. **2 N×Q, P—B7**, and White cannot prevent the pawn from queening.

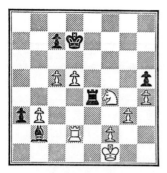

57. *Black to play*

The game from the position shown in Diagram 57 was lost by Buslaev, in a Russian team match, 1971. **1...P—R7** is correct. Buslaev blundered, trying for a brilliancy, with 1...R—K8 ch?; 2 K×R, B—B6; 3 K—Q1, B×R; 4 K—B2!, and Black resigned, as the white king stops the black pawn queening, and White wins with his extra pawns **2 R—Q1, B—B6**, threatening 3...R—K8 ch. The immediate 2...P—R8=Q; 3 R× Q, B×R is not so good, because after 4 N×P, White's pawns are dangerous. **3 N—K2, P—R8=Q; 4 R×Q, B×R**, and Black wins.

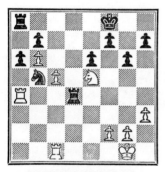

58. Balashov *v* Bronstein (U.S.S.R. Youth team *v* U.S.S.R. 2nd team, 1973) *White to play*

The position in Diagram 58 contains a complex tactical idea, but the clue lies in White's pawns on the fifth and sixth ranks. There is plenty of material on the board, but these pawns are far enough advanced to allow Balashov a win by promotion tactics. **1 P—B6!!**, P×P. If 1...R×R, then 2 P×P, and White rapidly queens, irrespective of what Black does. **2 R×R, N×R; 3 P—N7, R—Q1; 4 N×QBP**, and now the game finished off rapidly. **4...N×N; 5 R×N, K—K2; 6 R—B8, R—Q8 ch; 7 K—R2, Black resigns.**

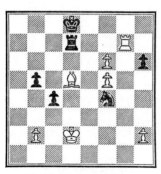

59. Najdorf *v* Stahlberg (Candidates', *Zurich*, 1953) *White to play*

In Diagram 59 White does not appear to have an easy way of forcing a pawn through. His bishop is pinned, and he must exchange rooks, since 1 P—B7, R×B ch; 2 K moves, R×P, is clearly good for Black. **1 R×R ch, K×R.** Now it seems that Black's king and knight can combine together to attack the white KB pawns, but...**2 B—B6 ch!**, and **Black resigns.** If the bishop is captured, then the black king is drawn too far away from the KB file to prevent the forward KBP from queening (the knight is clearly powerless), while if 2...K—Q1 (intending, if 3 P—B7, to play K—K2), then simply 3 B×P, which begins a mopping-up operation against all Black's pawns.

60. Karasev *v* Geller
(U.S.S.R. Championship, 1971)
Black to play

61. Karolyne *v* Ivanka
(Women's Championship,
Budapest, 1972)
White to play

62. Euwe *v* Averbakh
(Candidates', *Zurich*, 1953)
Black to play

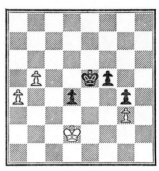

63. Stoltz *v* Nimzowitsch
(*Berlin*, 1928)
Black to play

See Diagram 60. **1...P—B5!; 2 P—R4.** Or 2 K—B4, P—N5; 3 K—N4, P—K5!; 4 P×(either)P, P—B6, and Black queens. **2...P×P; 3 K—B4, P—K5!, and White resigns,** for if 4 P×P, P—B6; 5 P×P, P—R6, then Black's KRP queens.

Ivanka, who won the tournament with ease, was very lucky to scrape a half point from Diagram 61. After 1 K—Q2?, K×P; 2 B—N7, K—Q4; 3 B—B3, a draw was agreed. The move that White missed was **1 B×P ch!**, decoying the king away from the passed pawns. The king and pawn ending after 1...K×P; 2 B×B, would be a simple win for White. **1...K×B; 2 P—B6!.** Black's bishop is unable to stop both pawns.

Black stands better in Diagram 62. White's bishop is very bad, relegated to the function of a pawn (and one which has little hope of improving its status). The president-to-be of the Soviet Chess Federation, facing the president-to-be of the World Chess Federation, found a neat way of forcing a pawn through on the queen's side by **1...N×RP!; 2 B×N, N—N4; 3 B—B1.** Or 3 B—N2, P—R6. **3...N×BP; 4 N—K2, N—N8!,** and White cannot prevent at least one of the pawns queening.

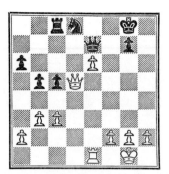

64. Lewis *v* Rubin (*South Africa*, 1962)
White to play

From Diagram 63, Black, originator of the concept that pawns have an in-built lust to expand, wins thanks to a pawn breakthrough: **1...P—B5!; 2 P×P ch, K—Q3!.** Nimzowitsch must not play 2...K—Q4; 3 P—B5, P—N6; 4 P—B6, K—K3; 5 P—N6, P—N7; 6 P—N7, P—N8=Q; 7 P—N8=Q, as White escapes with a draw. After 2...K—Q3; Black's king holds up the advance of the white pawns long enough for one of his own to be forced through to queen: **3 P—R5, P—N6; 4 P—R6, K—B2; 5 K—K2, P—Q6 ch!; 6 K×P, P—N7, White resigns.**

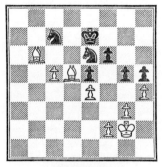

65. Etmans *v* Tilstra
(*Holland*, 1967)
White to play

The black position (Diagram 64) is restricted, so that Black's extra piece has very little freedom of movement. The pawn can be forced home after **1 Q—Q7!, R—B2.** If 1...Q×Q, then 2 P×Q, R—R1; 3 R—K8 ch, followed by the advance of White's king's-side pawn majority. **2 Q×R!, Q×Q; 3 P—K7,** and wins.

White, in Diagram 65, has a distant passed pawn but finds it impossible to make any progress, so...he creates another! **1 B(6)×N!, N×B; 2 P—N4!, RP×P; 3 P—R5, K—B1; 4 P—R6, N—R3; 5 P—B6, N—B2; 6 K—N3,** and the white king gobbles up the leading NP, and then...gobbles up all the other black pawns.

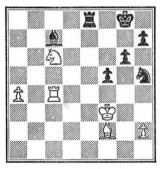

66. Korchnoi *v* Mecking
(7th match game, 1974)
White to play

This example (Diagram 66) virtually decided a world championship candidates' quarter-final match, and shows that a passed pawn as far back as the fourth rank can quickly become decisive when other pieces are in support. **1 P—R5, B×KRP?.** Black should try 1...B×QRP; 2 N×B, P—N4, when a win for White would still be difficult, due to the reduction in material. **2 P—R6, K—B2; 3 P—R7, R—QR1; 4 R—Q4, P—N4; 5 R—Q8!,** and wins, since Black now has to surrender a full rook for the passed pawn.

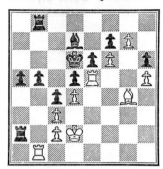

67. Panov *v* Zagoryansky
(*Moscow*, 1944)
White to play

See Diagram 67. **1 R—N5!, P×R.** Or
1...R—N1; 2 R—N6!, followed by
3 R×RP, or if 2...P×R, then 3 P×P,
4 P—B7, and 5 P—B8=Q. **2 P—R6,
P—N5; 3 P—R7, P×P ch; 4 K—B1,
R(7)—N7; 5 R×R, P×R ch; 6 K—N1,
B—R5; 7 B—Q1!.**
But not 7 P—R8=Q, B×P ch!, and
Black's queen will prove herself the
more effective (compare the comment at
the end of example 52). **7...P—B6;
8 P—R8=Q ,Black resigns.**

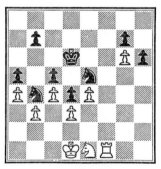

68. Kovacevic *v* Gliksman
(*Zagreb*, 1967)
White to play

Black, though the exchange down,

appears to have excellent drawing
chances in Diagram 68, but if he was
counting on these, then he received a
very rude awakening: **1 R—B6 ch!, K—
K2.** 1...P×R fails simply to the
advance of the KNP. **2 R—N6, P—R4;
3 K—K2.** Preparing to intercept the
RP. **3...P—R5; 4 R×P ch, K—B3; 5
R—N6 ch, K—N4; 6 R×N!, and Black
resigns.** If 6...BP×R, then 7 N—B3 ch,
N×N; 8 K×N, and White's passed
pawns carry all before them.

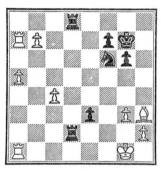

69. Langeweg *v* Wade
(England *v* Holland, 1971)
White to play

When both sides have a pawn close
to queening, the play is trappy (see
Diagrams 52 and 67). The position in
Diagram 69 was also the decisive game
in a match to qualify for the final of the
European team championship, which
helps to explain why White errs: **1 R—
K1?.** The winning move was 1 R—R8!,
and if 1...R—Q8 ch, then 2 R×R,
R×R ch; 3 K—N2, P—K7; 4 P—N8=
Q, R—N8 ch; 5 K—B3!, P—K8=Q;
6 Q—R8 mate. **1...R—Q8!; 2 K—B1.**
Now if 2 R×R, R×R ch; 3 K—N2,
Black is a tempo up on the previous
note, and wins by 3...P—K7; 4 P—
N8=Q, P—K8=Q, when White has no
good checks.
2...R(1)—Q7; 3 R×R, P—K7 ch!,
and **White resigns.**

4

WINNING AND DRAWING TECHNIQUES

'I lost, but the ending was drawn' and 'the ending was won, but I only drew' are two sayings frequently heard after club and tournament games.

The knowledge of a few basic winning and drawing techniques does much to help avoid needlessly dropping half-points, and also to help acquire extra half-points.

The diagrams in this chapter illustrate how draws may be saved or games won in four simple types of ending: (*a*) queen versus pawn on the seventh rank; (*b*) bishop and RP of the wrong colour; (*c*) bad bishop handicapped by its own pawns; and (*d*) stalemate traps.

Queen versus pawn on the seventh rank

This type of ending occurs only rarely, but it is well worth knowing the basic ideas behind it, if one is to avoid the acute embarrassment of only drawing a won position, with a queen up! See Diagram 70.

70. *White to play*

The basic winning technique was known by the end of the eighteenth century, and is here demonstrated by the greatest player of that era, namely Philidor.

1 Q—KB8 ch	K—N7
2 Q—N4	K—B7
3 Q—B4 ch	K—N7

| 4 Q—K3 | K—B8 |

Black's compulsion to protect his pawn is at the heart of this ending. White can always (except in some cases with RP or BP), force the black king to protect his pawn by occupying the queening square, and thus allowing the white king time to approach.

| 5 Q—B3 ch! | K—K8 |

Now Black is no longer threatening to queen his pawn immediately, so White can bring his king one step nearer.

| 6 K—N6! | K—Q7 |

Now White must repeat the process.

| 7 Q—B7 | K—Q8 |

If 7...Q—K6, then 8 Q—K1 simplifies White's task.

8 Q—Q4 ch	K—B7
9 Q—K3	K—Q8
10 Q—Q3 ch	

Again the black king is forced to occupy the queening square.

| 10 . . . | K—K8 |
| 11 K—B5 | |

And again the white king is able to move one square closer. Once more the merry-go-round gets under way:

11 . . .	K—B7
12 Q—Q2	K—B8
13 Q—B4 ch	K—N8
14 Q—K3 ch	K—B8
15 Q—B3 ch	K—K8
16 K—Q4	K—Q7
17 Q—QB3 ch	

17 Q—Q3 ch, K—K8; 18 K—K3, also wins, but the text reveals a useful mating idea.

| 17 . . . | K—Q8 |
| 18 K—Q3 | P—K8=Q |

Black is finally allowed to queen, but only at the cost of:

19 Q—B2 or Q—R1 mate

The win in the above example is quite simple, but with BP or RP it is not so simple, and the inferior side can often draw. Look at Diagram 71.

71. *White to play*

From the previous example we know that White should now play:

1 Q—N3 ch

To force the king in front of the pawn, but in this case the confines of the board intrude. Black can simply play:

| 1 . . . | K—R8 |

Black draws, as 2 Q×P is stalemate – a problem which does not arise with a centre pawn, because then Black is always left with a move.

However, with White's king closer, mating positions similar to that in Diagram 70 become possible.

72. *White to play*

Diagram 72 shows such a case:

1 Q—N3!

Black's king must be prevented from escaping to the queen's side, when the position is drawn, as in the preceding example.

| 1 . . . | K—Q7 |

1...K—B8, simply allows White's king to approach one step nearer.

| 2 Q—N2 | K—Q8 |

Black's only hope is to repeat the threat to queen his pawn.

| 3 K—B3! | K—Q7 |

For if 3...P—B8=Q, then 4 Q—K2 mate.

| 4 K—B2 | K—Q8 |
| 5 Q—Q4 ch | |

In order to engineer a position in

which White will simultaneously prevent the black king from escaping to the queen's side and, at the same time, threaten mate.

5 . . .	K—B8
6 Q—QN4	K—Q8
7 Q—K1 mate	

Bishop and RP of the wrong colour

The term 'bishop and RP of the wrong colour' needs some explanation. It does not mean, as it appears to, that White has a bishop and Black a RP, but that one side has a bishop and a RP whose queening square is a different colour to that of the bishop.

The great danger for the superior side in this type of ending is, that the inferior side's king may be able to reach the queening square and, by oscillating between R1 and N2, obtain a draw. This is demonstrated in Diagram 73.

73. *Black to play*

Black simply plays 1...K—N2, and White is unable, without reaching a stalemate position, to prevent the king from moving between R1 and N2.

It seems that the black king in Diagram 74 can reach his KN2 without much trouble, but with White to move, a neat manoeuvre is available to prevent this:

1 B—K6!

Immediately cutting off one line of approach.

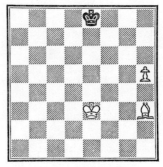

74. Troitsky (1896)
White to play

1 . . .	K—K2

If 1...K—B1, then 2 P—R6, and Black's king can make no further progress. White wins easily by advancing his own king.

2 P—R6! K—B3

Of course, Black cannot capture the bishop, as it allows the pawn a head start towards the queening square. It is this subtlety that allows White to win this position.

3 B—B5!

The bishop can be freely offered.

3 . . .   K—B2
4 B—R7!

Now that the king has been forced to go the other way it must be prevented from creeping along the back rank.

4 . . .   K—B3
5 K—B4   K—B2
6 K—B5

The 'opposition' has temporarily taken over as the most important factor. White is able to advance towards the pawn while forcing the black king away.

6 . . .   K—K2
7 K—N6   K—B1
8 K—B6   K—K1
9 K—N7 and wins

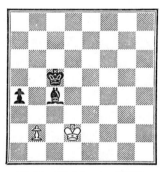

75. Von Holzhausen (1910)
White to play

The interest of this position (Diagram 75) is that White's pawn is a serious handicap – it prevents the white king from occupying his QN2 square, with an easy draw.

1 K—B2!

Alternatives lose: 1 K—B1?, B—Q6; 2 K—Q2, K—N5! and Black wins; while 1 K—B3? loses to 1...B—N6; 2 K—Q2 (or 2 K—Q3, K—N5; 3 K—Q2, K—B5); 2...K—B5!; 3 K—B1, B—R7; 4 K—B2 (or here 4 K—Q2, B—N8; 5 K—B1, B—N3); 4...K—N5; 5 P—N3, P—R6!

1 . . .   B—R7!

Black has to prevent the white king from reaching QR1, if he is to preserve any winning chances.

2 P—N4 ch!

The only move. 2 K—B1? and 2 K—Q2? lose to 2...K—B5!, and 2 K—B3? loses to 2...B—N6!; while 2 K—Q3? also loses to 2...B—N6!, e.g. 3 K—B3, K—N4; 4 K—Q2, K—B5.

2 . . .   K—any

2...P×P e.p.ch, also leads only to a draw, e.g. 3 K—N2, K—N5; 4 K—R1, and if Black tries to make any progress with 4...K—R6 or 4...K—B6, the result is stalemate.

3 K—N2

The white king reaches QR1 and draws.

Bad bishop handicapped by its own pawns

The significance of the 'bad' bishop is that its mobility is handicapped by its own pawns, which occupy squares of the same colour as the bishop. The pawns offer targets for the concerted action of the opposing king and bishop and frequently reduce the handicapped bishop to the role of a mere pawn, in that it can be used only to protect another pawn (at best two pawns).

The player with the better bishop should try to prevent the inferior side from making pawn breaks, which would help to free the position of the stifled bishop, or, allow the king to start a counter-attack. Once this task is accomplished the superior side will then set about finding objects of attack, preferably on opposite wings, so as to provide the defender with the maximum difficulty.

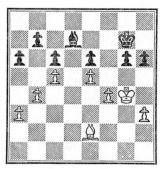

76. Baslavsky *v* Kondratiev
(U.S.S.R. Navy Championship,
1942)
White to play

In this position (Diagram 76), Black's bishop is very bad indeed. Its only chance to escape from its own constricting pawns lies in freeing the KN3 square by the advance ...P—KN4.

1 P—KR4

Preventing Black's one hope of liberation. Now White's king is free to go to the queen's side.

1 ...	B—K1
2 B—Q3	B—Q2
3 K—B3	P—KR4?

Black's position is very difficult, and the strain of holding it together tells. He should have preserved the threat of ...P—KN4, which represented his only possible counterchance.

Now it is quite easy for White: 4 K—K3, K—B2; 5 K—Q4, B—K1; 6 K—B3, K—K2; 7 K—N3, K—Q1; 8 K—R4, K—B2; 9 K—R5, B—B2; 10 B—B4. Zugzwang – the bishop has to go to N1. 10...B—N1; 11 P—R4, B—B2; 12 P—N5, RP×P; 13 P×P, B—N1. Or 13... P×P; 14 B×NP, and either White's bishop, or his king, penetrates into the heart of Black's position. **14 P—N6 ch,** K—Q1; **15 K—N4, B—B2; 16 K—B3,**

K—Q2; **17 K—Q4, P—N4.** Despair. If 17...K—K2; 18 K—K3, K—Q2; 19 P—B5 , NP×P; 20 K—B4, and White's king penetrates. **18 BP×P, B—N3; 19 K—K3, B—B7; 20 P—N6, B×P; 21 K—B4, B—B4; 22 B—K2, White wins.**

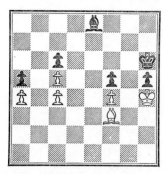

77. Schelfhout *v* Menchik
White to play

Black's bishop in Diagram 77 has two pawns to defend, and only a limited amount of space in which to manoeuvre. The task quickly proves too difficult: **1 B—N2, B—Q2; 2 B—R1, B—K1; 3 B—B3, B—Q2.** Or 3...B—B2; 4 B×BP, B×P; 5 B—K8!, B—N6; 6 P—B6, B×P; 7 P—B7, and wins. **4 B×RP, B—B1.** Or, here, 4...B—K3; 5 B—K8. **5 B—K8, B—N2; 6 B—Q7, K—N3; 7 K—N3, K—B3; 8 K—B3, K—N3; 9 K—K3, K—B3; 10 K—Q4, B—R1; 11 B—B8, K—K2; 12 K—K5,** and the rest is simple.

Here in Diagram 78 it is White's bishop that is severely restricted by its own pawns, and also by the need to guard against the threat of ...B×NP, should his bishop move back to KB2 or

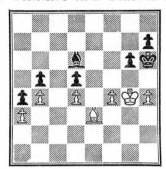

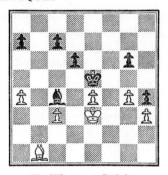

78. Kashlyaev *v* Zagoryansky
(Moscow Championship semi-final)
Black to play

79. Winawer *v* Steinitz
(*Vienna*, 1882)
Black to play

KN1, and thus be unable to prevent Black's QRP from queening.

1 ...	K—N2
2 P—B5	

The only way to continue the game, since 2 P—R5 allows 2...P×P ch, and the outside passed pawn decides.

2 ...	P—R4 ch
3 K—N5	B—K2 ch
4 K—B4	K—B3
5 P×P	B—Q3 ch

The white bishop can only observe the B1—R6 diagonal because of the threat of ...B×NP.

6 K—B3	K×P
7 B—B4	

If 7 B—N5, then 7...K—B4; 8 B—Q8, and Black's bishop attacks the pawns, and enables his king to penetrate to K5 or KN5.

7 ...	B—K2
8 B—N3	B—B3
9 B—B2	K—B4
10 Resigns	

White felt unable to prolong the game in view of the unavoidable loss of material. The black king's invasion will win either the QP or KRP.

In Diagram 79 White's bishop is bad, but it does have chances of coming to

life on the R2—N8 and B1—R6 diagonals. Steinitz's technique is impressive:

1 ...	B—B8
2 K—B3	P—N4!

Black should not play 2...B×P, which allows White to go in for 3 B—Q3!, K—B3; 4 K—B4, B—N7; 5 P—N5 ch, K—K3; 6 B—B4 ch, K—K2; 7 B—Q3, P—R6; 8 K—N3, K—K3; 9 P—K5, with good counterchances.

3 B—R2	P—B3

Threatening 4...B—Q6, winning KP

4 B—B7

Or 4 B—N1, P—R4; 5 B—B2, B—B5, and Black wins a pawn because White's bishop is in zugzwang.

4 ...	B—Q6
5 K—B2	

If 5 B—N6, then 5...P—Q4 wins the pawn.

5 ...	K—B5
6 P—R5	B×P
7 B—B4	P—Q4

Now the rest is easy: 8 B—R6, P—B4; 9 B—B8, P—B5; 10 P—R6, K—K4; 11 B—Q7. Or 11 K—K3, B—N7. 11...P—Q5; 12 P×P ch, K×P; 13 K—K2, B—Q6 ch; 14 K—K1, P—B6; 15 B—B8, K—K6; 16 K—Q1, K—B7; 17 B—B5, B×P; 18 K—B2, B—B8; 19 K×P, B×P, and Black soon queens.

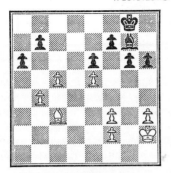

80. Van Scheltinga *v* Fine
(*Amsterdam*, 1936)
Black to play

In this position (Diagram 80) White is not only saddled with a bad bishop, but his pawns are so weak that they present an easy target for the black king: 1...K—B1; 2 K—N3, K—K1; 3 K—B4, K—Q2; 4 K—K4, K—B3; 5 K—Q4, K—N4; 6 B—Q2, P—KR4; 7 P—B4, B—B1; 8 P—B3, P—R4; 8 Resigns, because he must immediately lose one pawn, and more would follow.

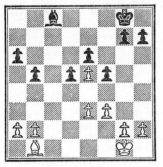

81. Penrose *v* Winter
(British Championship, 1950)
White to play

Black's bishop is a bad one in Diagram 81, but the pawn formation is not yet completely fixed, thus providing the bishop with some hope of escape.

1 P—QN4!

Fixing Black's queen's-side pawns on (for Black) disagreeable light squares.

1 ...	K—B2
2 K—B2	B—N2
3 B—B2	K—K2
4 B—N3	

With the pawn formation fixed, White has plenty of time to improve the position of his pieces.

4 ...	K—Q2
5 K—K2	B—B1
6 K—Q3	K—B2
7 K—Q4	

Completing the process of centralization, and introducing the real threat of penetration into Black's position.

| 7 ... | K—N3 |
| 8 P—KR3 | P—KR4 |

Another black pawn reaches a light square, but ...P—N4 and ...P—R3 represents no improvement.

| 9 P—N3 | P—N4 |
| 10 P—KR4 | P×P |

Not 10...P—N5; 11 P×P, BP×P; 12 B—B2—N6, or 11...RP×P; 12 P—R5, and the pawn queens.

11 P×P	B—Q2
12 B—B2	B—B3
13 B—Q1	B—K1
14 P—K4	

The decisive breakthrough.

| 14 ... | QP×P |
| 15 P×P | P×P |

If 15...P—B5, then the white king transfers to KB3 with an easy victory.

16 K×P	K—B3
17 B—B3	K—B2
18 K—B4	B—B3
19 B×B	Resigns

Further resistance is useless, e.g. 19...K×B; 20 K—N5, K—Q4; 21 K—B6.

Stalemate traps

The examples in this section contain a clear moral—*do not resign too quickly.* This is not to advocate playing on, with a large amount of material down, right up until mate, but rather that before resigning, it is worthwhile having a good look at the position just to check that there isn't a surprising resource. This is in order if your king has only a very few moves available, and especially so if it is already in a 'stalemate' position, as in Diagrams 82 and 85.

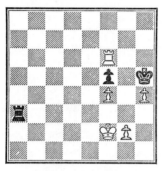

82. Reshevsky *v* Geller
(Candidates', *Zurich*, 1953)
White to play

Black's position in Diagram 82 with one pawn against three is apparently hopeless, but even with White to move a draw results.

1 P—N3

Or 1 R×P ch, K×P, and now 2 R—B8, K—N5, and Black regains a pawn or gets perpetual check; or 2 R—KN5, R—R7 ch; 3 K—N1, R—R8 ch; 4 K—R2, R—R8 ch; 5 K×R, stalemate.

1 . . .   **R—B6 ch**
2 Draw agreed

For example, 2 K—N2, R×NP ch; 3 K×R is stalemate, and if White does not take the rook, Black has an easily drawn rook and pawn ending.

The alternative of perpetual check or stalemate, if the rook is captured, is a particularly common theme, to which the above example serves as an intro-duction, but which can be seen in purer form in Diagrams 84 and 85.

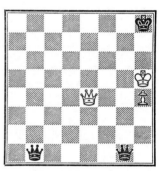

83. Dikarev *v* Pelts
(*Ukraine*, 1964)
White to play

In Diagram 83, White, a queen down, seems helpless, and Dikarev certainly believed that no further resistance was possible. White played 1 Q—R8 ch, and resigned after 1...Q—KN1. Instead he could have snatched a draw with:

1 Q—K5 ch!   **K—R2(N1)**

If 1...Q—KN2, then 2 Q—N8 ch! restores material equilibrium, or results in stalemate.

2 Q—N7 ch!   **Q×Q**
                        stalemate

If 2...K×Q, this produces an identical result.

84. Tomovic *v* Vidmar
(*Ljubljana,* 1945–46)
White to play

Here (Diagram 84), White is only one pawn ahead, but he has a much better position, and should win easily.

1 K—Q6?

White wins with very little trouble after 1 R—K7!, R—Q8; 2 R—K8, R—Q7; 3 P—B6!, K—N3; 4 R—N8 ch, K—R3; 5 P—K6!, and the pawn breakthrough is decisive.

1 . . .   R×P!!

Black surprisingly escapes.

2 K×R   P—B3 ch

Whether White captures the pawn or moves his king, is irrelevant, because Black has no more moves and it is stalemate.

White has an easy win in Diagram 85, but Matulovic was apparently oblivious

85. Matulovic *v* Suttles
(Interzonal, *Palma,* 1970)
White to play

to the fact that Black's king is stalemated, and calmly played . . .

1 K—B2??

1 N—Q5, leaving the black king able to move, wins easily.

1 . . .   R—Q7 ch

The position is now drawn. Matulovic, as is his wont, continued to the bitter end.

2 K—K1

Or 2 K—K3, R—Q6 ch; 3 K—any, R×P!, and the draw is clear.

2 . . .   R—K7 ch
3 K—B1   R—KB7 ch
4 K—N1   R—KN7 ch

The only way for White to escape the perpetual check is to capture the rook, and that results in stalemate.

5 K—R1   R—KR7 ch
6 K×R   stalemate

PART TWO

ENDGAMES FOR
TOURNAMENT AND
MATCH PLAYERS

5

ROOK ENDGAMES

The key principle of rook endgames is to seek active and aggressive positions for your own rook and king, and to drive your opponent's rook and king on to the defensive. This means making use of the fact that rooks are specially strong on open files, and even on open ranks. In attacking enemy pawns, they are most effective from the rear. Rooks are weakest when tied to the protection of a pawn, and a frequent motif for a player in difficulties in a rook endgame is to sacrifice a pawn, so as to bring his rook from a passive to an active position.

The best of all active rook positions is on the seventh rank, cutting off the opponent's king on the back row – what Nimzowitsch called 'the absolute seventh'. If, in addition to the absolute seventh, a player has a passed pawn supported by the king, then he is in a position to set up mating threats, which may more than compensate for being one or more pawns down.

Simple rook endgames where the superior side has one pawn against none, or two against one, have in many cases been analysed out to a win or draw. This chapter will not attempt to cover the full range of these basic endings. Practical players will often find that the relevant positions occur sufficiently near to adjudication or adjournment time for an exactly similar instance to be tracked down. The recommended procedure is to refer to either Reuben Fine's *Basic Chess Endings* or David Hooper's *A Pocket Guide to Endgames*, and to look up the correct play before your own game resumes, or is adjudicated. Then, after the game is over, but while your interest remains fresh, play through and try to absorb some of the rules and principles which govern similar basic positions. This method means that the learning process in the tough subject of theoretical rook endgames occurs when the player is highly motivated to absorb material. Few players have the exceptional mental discipline required to learn theoretical rook endgames in the abstract, without the incentive of a possible tournament or match point.

This chapter discusses (*a*) active rook versus passive rook; (*b*) the active king; (*c*) pawn races; (*d*) the Philidor and Lucena positions; (*e*) tactical decisions; and (*f*) rook against minor piece. All these themes are worth study as fundamental ideas which continually occur in rook endgames.

Active rook versus passive rook

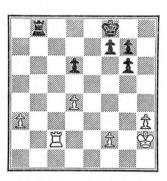

86. Spielmann *v* Rubinstein
(*St Petersburg*, 1909)
Black to play

In Diagram 86 it looks, superficially, as though White has the advantage, because of his outside passed RP, but Rubinstein, the greatest ever exponent of rook endgames, finds a way to seize the initiative.

1 ...	R—R1
2 R—B3	R—R5
3 R—Q3	K—K2

Black now has an active against a passive rook. True, his rook is blockading the RP from the front, rather than in the ideal position from behind; but this is more than compensated by Black's extra space. As a general rule, a rook blockade from the front, is effective enough to create an active-passive rook situation, if the blockader is on the fifth or sixth rank.

4 K—N3

No better is 4 P—Q5, P—N4; 5 K—N2, K—B3; 6 R—B3 ch, K—N3; 7 R—Q3, P—B3, followed by K—B4—K4, and Black's king penetrates.

4 ...	K—K3
5 K—B3	K—Q4
6 K—K2	P—N4!

Not 6...R×QP?; 7 K—K3!, R× R ch; 8 K×R, when the QRP gives

White a guarantee of at least a draw.

7 R—QN3	P—B3
8 K—K3	K—B5
9 R—Q3	P—Q4
10 K—Q2	R—R1
11 K—B2	R—R2
12 K—Q2	R—K2

Putting White into zugzwang, for if 13 R—K3, then 13...R—N2; 14 R—Q3, R—N7 ch; 15 K—K3, R×P. Spielmann therefore tries the resource, mentioned in the introduction to this chapter, of sacrificing a pawn so as to bring his rook to a more active position in support of the RP.

13 R—B3 ch	K×P
14 P—QR4	R—R2
15 R—R3	R—R4
16 R—R1	K—B5
17 K—K3	P—Q5 ch
18 K—Q2	R—KB4!
19 K—K1	K—N5
20 K—K2	K—R4

Black has reactivated his rook, while the white rook still has little scope. The remaining moves show Rubinstein cleverly cashing in on his material advantage: 21 R—R3, R—B5; 22 R—R2, R—R5; 23 K—Q3, R×P ch; 24 K×P, R—R5 ch; 25 K—Q3, R×P; 26 R—K2, R—KB5; 27 K—K3, K—N3; 28 R—B2, K—N2; 29 R—B1, R—QR5; 30 R—KR1, K—B3; 31 R—R7, R—R2; 32 K—K4, K—Q3; 33 K—B5, P—N3 ch; 34 K×NP, R×R; 35 K×R, K—K4; 36 K—N6, P—N5; White resigns.

Black stands slightly better in Diagram 87, because his rook is more active. This advantage should not be sufficient for a win here, but it is a characteristic of rook endgames, as of chess in general, that a player with White who has lost the initiative, may

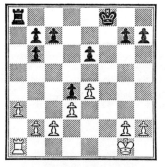

87. Marshall v Tarrasch
(7th match game, 1905)
White to play

become discouraged and commit further inaccuracies.

1 R—B1 ch	K—K2
2 R—B4	

Not the best. White should play his king over to Q2.

2 ...	R—R4!

Black sets about weakening White's queen's-side pawns.

3 K—B1

Not 3 P—K5, R×KP; 4 R×P, R—K7; 5 R—QB4, P—B4, when Black's rook on the seventh rank is a formidable piece.

3 ...	R—QB4
4 R—B2	R—QN4
5 P—QN3	R—KR4

Gaining time to blockade the white QRP.

6 P—R3	P—QN4!
7 P—QN4?	

Creating another and more serious weakness, since the RP becomes backward and an ideal target for Black's blockading rook. Better is 7 K—K2.

7 ...	R—R3
8 R—B4	P—K4
9 R—B5	R—K3
10 K—K2	P—KN3
11 R—B1	R—R3
12 R—QR1	P—N3

13 K—Q2	R—R5
14 P—B3	

After this, Tarrasch has a forcing line, but the more natural 14 K—B1 is met by 14...R—R1!; 15 K—N2, R—KB1; 16 R—KN1, R—B7; 17 K—N3, K—K3.

14 ...	P—B4
15 P×QP	

If 15 P×BP, then 15...NP×P; 16 K—B2, P—B5!

15 ...	P×NP!

Black now gets a powerful outside RP, and maintains his basic active versus passive rook advantage. The game is decided: 16 P×KP, K—K3; 17 P—Q4, P×P; 18 K—B3, P—R7; 19 P—N4, P—N4; 20 K—Q3, P—N5; 21 K—B4, P—N6 dis ch; 22 K×P, R×P; 23 R×P, R×P; 24 R—R6, R—K6 ch; 25 K—B2, R×RP; 26 R×P ch, K×P; 27 R—N4, R—K6; 28 K—Q2, R—K5; **White resigns.**

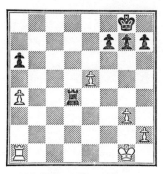

88. Dake v Campolongo
(*Folkestone*, 1933)
White to play

In Diagram 88, White can draw by activating his rook: 1 R—N1!, P—N3; 2 R—N8 ch, K—N2; 3 R—N7, K—B1; 4 R—N8 ch, K—K2; 5 R—N7 ch, K—K3; 6 R—N6 ch, etc. Instead he chose 1 K—B2?, when 1...R—K5; 2 K—B3, R×KP cost him a pawn and lost him the game.

89. Flohr *v* Vidmar
(*Nottingham*, 1936)
White to play

See Diagram 89. White's rook is active since it ties down the black rook and can be supported on its outpost square by P—QN4. In addition, a rook established in the opponent's half of the board has opportunities for manoeuvre along the rank, and this is one of the themes of Flohr's subsequent play.

1 K—K2	K—K2
2 K—Q3	K—Q3
3 R—R5	R—QR1
4 K—Q4	P—KB4
5 P—QN4	

Permanent prevention of any liberating pawn advance.

5 . . .	R—QN1
6 P—QR3	R—QR1

6. . .R—N3 leaves the rook completely immobilized.

7 P—K4!

Opening up the central squares for the king and the fifth rank for the rook.

7 . . .	BP×P
8 P×P	P×P
9 K×P	R—R2
10 K—B4	P—R3

Black cannot allow the white king to reach KR6 and eat up the king's-side pawns.

11 P—KR4	K—K3
12 K—N4	R—R1
13 P—R5!	

Fixing the king's-side pawns, and so creating a later possibility of winning Black's KRP and queening his own. The remaining moves show White's rook penetrating the black position, while the black rook is still denied any opportunity to become active: **13. . .P—N4; 14 P—N3, R—R2; 15 K—B3, R—R1; 16 K—K4, R—R2; 17 R—K5 ch, K—Q3; 18 R—K8, P—B4; 19 R—Q8 ch, K—B3; 20 R—B8 ch, K—N3; 21 R×P, R—R2; 22 R—K5, K—B3; 23 R—K6 ch, K—N4; 24 K—B5, R—B2 ch; 25 R—B6, Resigns.** Both Black's king's-side pawns will fall.

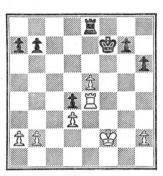

90. Capablanca *v* Reti
(*New York*, 1924)
White to play

In this position (Diagram 90), White's rook is active and Black's passive, because of the restraining effect of the passed KP. Capablanca utilizes this advantage to advance his king to a dominating square: **1 K—B3, R—Q1.** King moves are useless, e.g. 1. . .K—K3; 2 R×P!, or 1. . .K—N3; 2 R—N4 ch, K—B2; 3 R—B4 ch, K—N3; 4 K—K4. **2 R—N4,** both restraining Black's king, and bringing his own to K4. **2. . .P—KN4; 3 P—KR4!, K—N3; 4 P×P, P×P.** Black's passed pawn is insignificant. **5 K—K4, K—R4; 6 R—N1, K—R5; 7 P—K6, P—N5; 8 P—K7, Resigns.** A possible finish is 8. . .R—K1; 9 K—B5, R×P; 10 R×P ch, K—R6; 11 R×P, R—K7; 12 R—QN4, P—N3; 13 P—Q4, and White wins easily, because the black king is far distant.

The active king

Even when the defending side in a rook endgame has got his rook into active play, he can still lose if he allows the opponent's king too much scope for invasion. See Diagram 91.

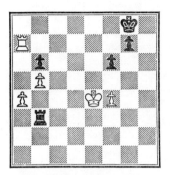

91. Kholmov *v* Vasyukov
(*Baku*, 1972)
Black to play

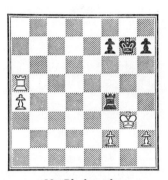

92. *Black to play*

Black's correct plan here is 1...R—N5 ch!, forcing the white king to stay guarding the KBP. Instead Black played 1...K—R2?; 2 K—Q5!. Now the white king threatens to grab the NP, after which White's united pawns win before Black can organize play with his own pawns. 2...R—QB6. Trying to keep out the king, but White's rook becomes active instead: 3 R—R6, R—B4 ch; 4 K—Q4, R—B4; 5 K—K3, P—N4; 6 R×P, R×BP; 7 P—R5, K—N3; 8 R—N8, R—QR5; 9 P—N6, R—R6 ch; 10 K—Q2, R—R7 ch; 11 K—Q3, R×P; 12 P—N7, K—B4; 13 R—QR8, R—N4; 14 P—N8=Q, R×Q; 15 R×R, K—B5; 16 K—K2, K—N6; 17 R—KB8, K—N7; 18 R×P, P—N5; 19 R—KN6, P—N6; 20 R—N8, Resigns.

The position in Diagram 92 was one submitted for adjudication in 1974. The original verdict was a draw, but White appealed on the grounds that 1...R—QN5; 2 R—N5 ch, K—B3; 3

R—N4, R—N7; 4 R—QB4, R—R7; 5 K—B3, R—R6 ch; 6 K—K4, followed by the king coming across to shepherd home the RP, should win.

Although this variation is not a sure win (Black has some play by winning White's KRP, and then advancing his own), it would be difficult for Black to fight against White's more active king. In practice, many rook endgames are decided because one player reacts too passively against a king march.

Black should therefore play more actively on the king's side in Diagram 92: 1...R—QN5; 2 R—N5 ch, K—B3; 3 R—N4, R—N6 ch!; 4 P—B3, P—R4!. An important move, because it puts Black one square nearer queening in the event of a pawn race. 5 R—QB4, K—B4; 6 P—R4. If 6 P—R3, then 6...R—R6; 7 R—B5 ch, K—N3; 8 P—R5, P—B3; 9 K—B4, R—R5 ch; 10 K—K3, P—R5, again with king's-side play. 6...R—R6; 7 R—B5 ch, K—N3; 8 P—R5, P—B3. Now if the white king marches to the queen's flank, Black wins the RP, after which his own RP, supported by the active king at KN3, is far enough advanced to ensure at least a draw. So the verdict of a draw was upheld.

Pawn races

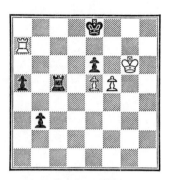

93. Taimanov *v* Belyavsky
(*Sukhumi*, 1972)
Black to play

In Diagram 93, Black is a pawn ahead and also has a lead in the race to queen. But White has his rook in the ideal position on the seventh rank, and also has his king and a potential passed pawn poised to join the attack. In such positions exact calculation is required, but it is all too easy to make mistakes, since this type of rook endgame is finely balanced between win, draw, and loss.

1 . . .	P—N7!

If 1...P×P, then 2 K—B6, P—N7; 3 P—K6, R—B1; 4 R—KR7, K—Q1; 5 R—Q7 ch at least draws, while if 1...R×P, then 2 P—B6, R—KB4; 3 R—QN7, R—KB6; 4 P—B7 ch, with perpetual check.

2 R—QN7	R—B7
3 K—B6?	

White could have drawn by 3 P—B6!, R—N7 ch; 4 K—R6, P—R5; 5 R—N8 ch, K—Q2; 6 P—B7, R—KB7; 7 R×P, R×P; 8 R—N7 ch, with perpetual check.

3 . . .	K—Q1!
4 K×P	

4 P×P is met by 4...R—B7 ch, and 5...P—R5.

4 . . .	P—R5
5 P—B6	P—R6
6 P—B7	R—B7
7 R—N3	K—B2
8 K—K7	R—B8
9 P—B8=Q	R×Q
10 K×R	P—R7
11 R×P	

If 11 P—K6, then 11...P—N8=Q; 12 P—K7, Q×R; 13 P—K8=Q, Q—QN1.

11 . . .	P—R8=Q
12 R—B2 ch	K—Q2
13 Resigns	

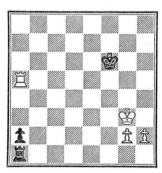

94. *White to play*

In simple pawn races where one player has two united passed pawns, and his opponent only one pawn, the stronger side normally wins if his king is in front of his pawns, and if his opponent cannot counter-attack. White wins in Diagram 94 by 1 P—R4, K—N3; 2 K—N4, K—B3; 3 R—R6 ch, K—B2; 4 K—R5, K—N2; 5 P—N4, K—B2; 6 R—R7 ch, K—K1; 7 P—N5, K—B1; 8 K—N6, giving up the RP, so as to win with the NP. 8...R—KR8; 9 R×P, R×P; 10 R—R8 ch, K—K2; 11 K—N7, and wins.

95. Rashkovsky *v* Smyslov
(U.S.S.R. Championship, 1973)
White to play

In this pawn race (see Diagram 95), Black's king supports his pawn, and gives him chances of counter-attack, while White's pawn advance has yet to start. Black can draw, but only by accurate play.

1 K—N3

Again the king should go in front of the pawns. Less effective is 1 P—N4, P—Q5; 2 P—B4, P—Q6; 3 R—K5 ch, K—Q3; 4 R—K3, K—Q4!; 5 P—B5, K—Q5; 6 R—K8, P—Q7; 7 R—Q8 ch, K—K6; 8 P—B6, P—Q8=Q; 9 R×Q,

R×R; 10 P—N5, R—KB8!, when it is White who has to fight to draw.

1 . . .	P—Q5
2 R—R8	K—Q4
3 P—B3	R—KB8!
4 K—B4	R—K8
5 P—N4	P—Q6
6 R—Q8 ch	K—B5
7 P—N5	R—KN8

7...K—B6? would lose to 8 P—N6, P—Q7; 9 P—N7, R—KN8; 10 K—K3, R—K8 ch; 11 K—B2.

8 K—K4

8 K—K3 is a closer try, but Black can still draw by 8...R—K8 ch!; 9 K—B2, R—K7 ch; 10 K—N3, R—K8; 11 P—B4, K—B6; 12 P—B5, P—Q7; 13 P—B6, R—K6 ch!; 14 K—R4, R—K5 ch!.

8 . . .	R—K8 ch
9 K—B5	K—B6
10 P—N6	R—KN8

Definitely saving the game, which concluded: **11 R—B8 ch, K—Q5; 12 K—B6, K—K6; 13 R—Q8, R—KB8!; 14 P—N7, R×P ch; 15 K—K5, R—KN6; 16 P—N8=Q, R×Q; 17 R×R, P—Q7; drawn.**

The Philidor and Lucena positions

These are the two basic rook and pawn endgame positions which it is essential for a practical player to know. Many rook endings ultimately boil down to rook and pawn against rook, and then it is a question whether the defender's king can blockade the pawn, as in Philidor's drawing method, or is cut off by the attacker's rook, as in the Lucena win.

96. Philidor's draw, discovered in 1777
White to play

Black maintains his rook on the third rank in Diagram 96, so as to hold back the white king. If the white pawn advances, Black moves his rook to the eighth rank to threaten checks on the files, and White, with his pawn committed to the sixth, cannot escape the checks: **1 P—K6, R—QR8; 2 K—B6, R—B8 ch; 3 K—K5, R—K8 ch; 4 K—Q6, R—Q8 ch** with a draw.

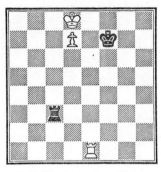

97. The Lucena position

The Lucena position is demonstrated in Diagram 97. White's rook makes a barrier which prevents the black king from approaching the pawn. The winning method is called 'building a bridge': **1 R—K4, R—B8.** If 1...K—B3, then 2 K—K8 wins. **2 R—B4 ch,** K—N2. If 2...K—N3, then 3 K—K8, R—K8 ch; 4 K—B8, R—Q8; 5 R—B7 wins. 3 K—K7, R—K8 ch; 4 K—Q6, R—Q8 ch; 5 K—B6, K—N3. If 5...R—B8 ch, then 6 K—Q5, R—Q8 ch; 7 R—Q4 completes the 'bridge-building' begun by 1 R—K4, and White wins. **6 R—QB4, K—B2; 7 K—B7, K—K2; 8 P—Q8=Q ch, R×Q; 9 R—K4 ch.**

Tactical decisions

The broad strategy of rook endgames is based on establishing an active rook and/or king, and on simplifying the endgame to one of the standard winning or drawing positions. But tactical and forcing variations can also play a part, as shown in Diagrams 98-102.

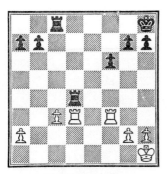

98. *Black to play*

Occasionally, at an early stage of a rook endgame, a king fails to emerge from the back rank quickly enough. Here in Diagram 98 **1...R×P!** wins at least a rook.

The zugzwang and triangulation themes (see Diagrams 42 and 105) in a rook endgame: Black won from Diagram 99 by **1...K—Q7!; 2 R—K4, K—B6; 3 R—R4, K—Q6,** and White's king must move, and allow the BP to queen. The tactical device here was made possible by the ultra-passive position of the white rook.

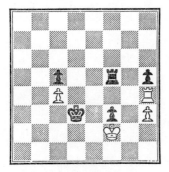

99. Tal *v* Spassky
(3rd match game, 1965)
Black to play

The tactical play from Diagram 100 is another instance of an ultra-passive rook. By conventional middle game standards, Black's rook at K4 is usefully centralized, but White's first move highlights its lack of mobility, which enables the QRP to run through: **1 P—N4!**, stopping ...R—R4; **1...R—K5; 2 P—R5, R×NP; 3 P—R6, R—N8.** If 3...R—R5, then 4 R—Q8, K×R; 5 P—R7. **4 P—R7, R—QR8; 5 R—QR3!, P×R; 6 P—R8=Q, P×P; 7 Q—N7 ch,** and wins.

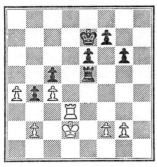

100. Won by Alekhine playing White
White to play

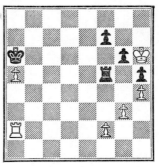

101. Alekhine *v* Capablanca
(34th match game, 1927)
White to play

Alekhine, again playing White in Diagram 101, eventually won by 1 P—B4, and the endgame books point out a triangulation manoeuvre winning a pawn after 1 K—N7, R—B6; 2 K—N8. But quicker still is the tactical win: **1 K—N7, R—B6; 2 R—Q2!, K×P; 3 R—Q5 ch,** and if 3...K—N3, then 4 R—Q6 ch, K—B4; 5 R—KB6; or 3...K—N5; 4 R—Q4 ch, K—B6; 5 R—KB4.

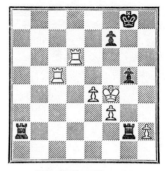

102. Szabo *v* Donner
(*Wageningen*, 1957)
White to play

From Diagram 102 Black seems to have good drawing chances, but Szabo uses tactical simplification to reach a standard win: **1 R×P ch, R×R; 2 K×R, R×P; 3 K—B6, R—R3 ch; 4 K—K7, R—R4.** If 4...R—R8; 5 R—Q8 ch, followed by 6 R—KB8. If 4...R—R6, then 5 R—KB6. **5 R—Q5!, Resigns.**

After 5...R—R2; 6 R—N5 ch, K—R1; 7 K—B8, R—R6; 8 R—KB5, White wins the BP and has two united pawns.

Rook against minor piece

This endgame, without pawns, is normally a draw, but in match practice it often occurs in a more complex form, where one side has avoided a middle game defeat at the price of a small material concession, such as a rook for minor piece and pawn.

The advantage of rook against bishop and pawn is usually harder to translate into a win than in the corresponding endgame with the knight, though a great deal depends on whether the bishop is mobile or restricted to defending its own pawn. A minor piece and two pawns against a rook, which is theoretically equal in the middle game, tends in the ending to favour the side with the pawns.

In all rook and pawn endings, the worst pawn to have is a RP, and this also applies in very simplified endings with rook against a minor piece.

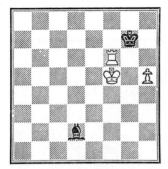

103. Tal v Zhidkov
(U.S.S.R. Championship, 1973)
White to play

Tal found the only possible winning method – to sacrifice the RP in order to drive the black king into a mating position: **1 P—R6 ch!, B×P.** Or 1... K—R2; 2 K—N4, B×P; 3 K—R5, B—N2; 4 R—B7 wins. **2 R—N6 ch, K—R2; 3 K—B6, B—K6; 4 K—B7, B—R2; 5 R—QR6, B—N1; 6 R—R8, B—B2; 7 R—QB8, B—B5; 8 R—B4, B—N4; 9 R—B3, Resigns.** If 9...B—Q7; or 9... K—R3, then 10 R—R3 ch, B—R3; 11 R—R5, K—R1; 12 R×B mate.

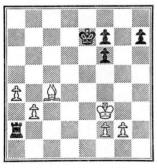

104. Spassky v Fischer
(21st match game, 1973)
White to play

The decisive game of the Spassky-Fischer match (see Diagram 104) was a typical case of a rook versus a minor piece ending, in which the rook's

advantage was slight. White has one pawn for the exchange, but the presence of doubled pawns means that he should be able to hold a draw with best play. Spassky's next move, however, lost him the endgame, and the world championship:

1 P—KN4?

Better is 1 P—N3, planning K—K3, P—B3, and careful control of the king side.

1 ...	P—B4!
2 P×P	P—B3
3 B—N8	P—R3

'This little pawn will win the world title,' commented a grandmaster who was watching.

| 4 K—N3 | K—Q3 |
| 5 K—B3? | |

5 P—B4, gives a better chance to erect a barrier preventing penetration by Black's king.

5 ...	R—R8
6 K—N2	K—K4
7 B—K6	K—B5
8 B—Q7	R—QN8
9 B—K6	R—N7
10 B—B4	R—R7
11 B—K6	P—R4?

11...K—N5!, followed by ...P—R4, is a simpler method.

12 B—Q7? and White resigned

After Spassky's mistake, 12...K—N5 wins by the threat of creating a mating net with ...P—R5—R6, e.g. 13 B—K6, P—R5; 14 B—Q7, P—R6 ch; 15 K—N1, R—R8 ch; 16 K—R2, R—KB8; 17 P—R5, R×P ch; 18 K—N1, K—N6; 19 P—R6, P—R7 ch; 20 K—R1, R—B8 mate.
12 K—R3! would have proved more difficult to overcome, but 12...R×BP; 13 P—R5, R—B8!; 14 P—R6, R—R8 ch; 15 K—N2, R—R8; 16 B—B4, K×P; 17 P—N4, K—K4!; 18 P—N5, K—Q3; 19 P—N6, K—B3; 20 P—N7, K—B2 achieves the desired end. The rook and two pawns can engineer the win on their own.

6

TEXTBOOK THEORY

Endgames have at least one factor in common with openings: the practical player has to select how much of an established body of theory he should know, or has time to know. To learn all the niceties of sharp variations in the Najdorf Sicilian is self-defeating. By the time the relevant position has been reached on the board, the player has probably forgotten the analysis. Similar situations occur in endgames when it comes to memorizing all the niceties of when rook or queen endings are won or drawn.

The other extreme is also wrong. To play a game, knowing little about the standard winning manoeuvres in knight or bishop endings, is just as much a weakness as regularly playing the Sicilian without being sure how to counter the Morra Gambit (1 P—K4, P—QB4; 2 P—Q4, P×P; 3 P—QB3). Even the match player whose endgames are often left to the adjudicator (chapter 9), can be helped by knowing frequently recurring won or drawn situations. Such knowledge can shape his approach and strategy in the last half-dozen moves before time is called, or even affect the decision whether to stop at, say move 48, or try to hustle the opponent into the next quarter-hour time control at move 54.

The aim of this chapter is to provide a basis of relevant, pure endgame knowledge, which will enable readers to pick up extra points or half points, and to help in middle game assessments as to whether to attack or simplify.

This chapter discusses (*a*) advanced techniques in pawn endgames; (*b*) knight endgames; (*c*) bishop endgames; (*d*) endgames of bishop against knight without rooks; and (*e*) queen endgames.

Advanced techniques in pawn endgames

The three techniques involved here, triangulation, the feint, and zugzwang, are among the most important situations for conducting an endgame well that a player can learn.

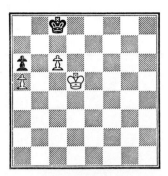

105. *White to play*

Diagram 105 shows triangulation at its simplest. White wins by **1 K—B4, K—Q1.** Or **1...K—N1. 2 K—Q4, K—B1; 3 K—Q5!**, completing the triangle.

106. *Black to play*

In Diagram 106, Black loses his pawn after **1...K—Q4.** Or **1...K—B5; 2 K—B2, K—K5; 3 K—N2**, going around via the queen's side. **2 K—K3.**

With White to play, he triangulates to get the same position, with Black to move: **1 K—Q1, K—Q4.** If **1...K—B5**, then **2 K—B2. 2 K—K2, K—K5; 3 K—Q2.**

In this example, Black's movements were restricted by the white QP controlling the K4 square.

107. *White to play*

From Diagram 107 comes a classic example of a feint, or diversion, in a pawn endgame, played by Lasker in his game against Tarrasch, St Petersburg, 1914. After **1 K—B6, P—B5; 2 P×P, P×P; 3 K—K5, P—B6; 4 P×P, P—R5,** White would lose because his retreat on the long diagonal is obstructed. So Lasker played the 'feint' **1 K—N6,** threatening to advance his KRP, **1...K×P; 2 K—B5,** and drew after **2...K—N6; 3 K—K4, K—B7; 4 K—Q5, K—K6; 5 K×P, K—Q6. Draw agreed.**

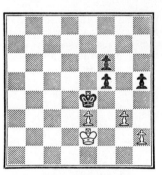

108. Flohr *v* Capablanca
(Moscow, 1935)
White to play

Here (see Diagram 108) ex-world champion Capablanca saves the game thanks to zugzwang. If it were Black's move he would be in zugzwang, able to make only losing moves: **1, .K—Q4;**

2 K—B3, K—K4; 3 P—R3, K—Q4; 4 K—B4, K—K3; 5 P—R4, and Black is again in zugzwang and, movebound, he must lose a pawn and the game.

But in the game it was White to move. He also is in zugzwang and can earn no more than a draw: 1 P—R3. The attempt to triangulate by 1 K—B2, fails to 1...P—R5; 2 P×P, P—B5. 1...K—Q4; 2 K—B3, K—K4. Since if 3 P—R4, K—Q4; 4 K—B4, K—K3, White is again in zugzwang and can make no progress.

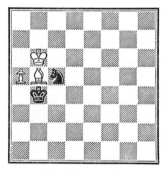

109. *White to play*

Diagram 109 shows another simple zugzwang position in an endgame with one piece on each side. If it is Black's move, he has to move his knight, and allow the pawn to queen, while White, to play, cannot force a recurrence of the same position, with his opponent to move: **1 B—B6, K—B5; 2 B—K8, K—Q5.** But not 2...K—N5?; 3 B—N5, when White has achieved a zugzwang. **3 B—B7, N—Q2 ch; 4 K—B6, N—N1 ch; 5 K—N5.** If 5 K—N7, then 5...K—B4; 6 B—K8, K—N5 draws. **5...K—B6; 6 B—K6, K—N7: 7 K—N6, K—R6; 8 K—N7, K—N5,** and White cannot force his pawn through to queen.

The idea of losing a move, or handing the move to the opponent, is a common one in endings, as we have already seen in the examples of triangulation.

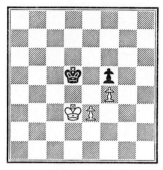

110. Szabo *v* Steiner
(*Groningen,* 1946)
Black to play

This example (Diagram 110) shows the 'opposition zugzwang,' another commonly recurring theme. With White to move, Black has the opposition and White cannot make progress: 1 K—B2, K—B3; 2 K—Q2, K—Q3, an example of the 'distant opposition,' with three squares between the kings. After 1 K—B2, Black could also draw with 1...K—Q3, but not 1...K—K5, because of 2 K—Q2, K—Q4; 3 K—Q3, and White has the opposition.

In the game it was Black's move, and Steiner resigned, because if 1...K—K3, then White takes opposition on the diagonal with 2 K—B4, and outflanks and wins Black's pawn after 2...K—Q3; 3 K—Q4, K—K3; 4 K—B5. If 1...K—Q3, then 2 K—Q4, with the same idea, and, finally, if 1...K—B4, then 2 P—K4, P×P ch; 3 K×P, K—Q3; 4 K—B5, and White's BP queens.

The example in Diagram 111 shows a rare situation: a zugzwang with a knight's move between the kings, sometimes called the *trébuchet*. A player forced to move because of zugzwang normally draws, while in the trébuchet the unlucky mover pays the full penalty. It is easy to see that whichever side moves has to lose his pawn, and allow the opposing king into a winning position in front of the remaining pawn.

Though this idea is rare, it does have

1 . . .	K—B2
2 K—B1	K—B3
3 K—Q2	K—K4

Step one.

4 K—K3	P—KR4
5 P—R3	P—R4

Step two, pinning down White's QNP, and threatening P—QR5, completely fixing the queen's side.

6 N—R3	N—B7 ch

116. *White to play*

7 K—B3

7 K—Q2, would have made Black's task harder, since 7...N×P; 8 P×N, K×P; 9 K—B3 leads to a clear draw. Black would retain good winning chances with 7...N—Q5; 8 K—K3, N—K3!, limiting the activity of White's knight and threatening to attack the KP.

7 . . .	N—K8 ch
8 K—K2	N—N7
9 K—B3	N—R5 ch
10 K—K3	N—N3
11 N—N5	K—B3
12 N—R7 ch	K—K2
13 N—N5	N—K4

Step three.

14 K—Q4	K—Q3
15 N—R3	

White cannot prevent the blockade of his queen's-side pawns.

15 . . .	P—QR5!
16 N—B4	P—R5
17 N—R3	P—N3!

Gaining an important tempo.

18 N—B4	P—N4
19 N—R3	N—B3 ch
20 K—K3	K—B4
21 K—Q3	P—N5

The attacker should usually avoid pawn exchanges, but Nimzowitsch has carefully calculated that this is a forced winning line.

22 P×P ch	K×P
23 K—B2	N—Q5 ch

Step four. White's king is driven as far away as possible from Black's KRP.

24 K—N1	N—K3
25 K—R2	K—B5!
26 K—R3	K—Q5
27 K×P	K×P
28 P—N4	

Also 28 N—N1, K—K6; and 29...K—B7; or 28 N—B2 ch, K—B6. Both win for Black.

28 . . .	K—B6

117. *White to play*

29 P—N5	K—N7
30 Resigns	

After 30 P—N6, K×N; 31 P—N7, N—B4 ch and wins the pawn; or 31 K—N5, N—Q1; 32 K—B5, K—N5; 33 K—Q6, P—R6; 34 K—B7, P—R7; 35 K×N, P—R8=Q, and wins.

Diagram 118 is another example (compare Diagram 114) in which White wins a knight ending because he has one piece better posted than Black. In the previous case White had the better

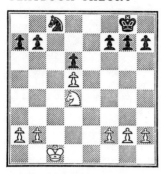

118. Alekhine *v* Andersen
(Olympiad, *Folkestone*, 1933)
White to play

king; here he has the better knight. It is
closer to the pawns and can force either
gain of material or a serious positional
weakness.
The decisive manoeuvre is:

1 N—N3 !　　　K—B1

Black's king is too far away from the
queen's side to leave him with a choice,
e.g. 1...N—K2; 2 N—R5, N×P; 3
N×P, N—B5; 4 N×P, N—Q6 ch; 5
K—B2, N×BP; 6 P—QN4!, K—B1; 7
P—QR4, and if 7...K—K2, then 8
N—B8 ch, while after 7...N—N5; 8
P—N5, N×P; 9 P—R5, the QRP cannot

be stopped from queening.

2 N—R5	P—QN3
3 N—B6	K—K1
4 K—Q2	N—K2

Black must prevent the approach of
the white king.

5 N×P	N×P
6 N—N5	

Alekhine has thus transformed his
original superior knight position into
the more lasting advantage of an outside
passed pawn.

6 ...	K—Q2
7 N—Q4	P—N3
8 P—QR4	N—B2
9 K—B3	P—KN4
10 K—N4	P—Q4
11 N—B3	P—B3
12 N—Q4	K—Q3

This only hastens the end, but Black
is also hopelessly lost after 12...K—
K2; 13 P—R5, P×P ch; 14 K×P, K—
Q2; 15 P—QN4, K—B1; 16 K—N6.

13 N—N5 ch	N×N
14 K×N	K—K4
15 P—QN4	P—Q5
16 K—B4	Resigns

Bishop endgames

Bishop endings can be divided into two main groups: bishops of the
same colour and bishops of opposite colour. When bishops are of the
same colour, a lead of two pawns is a win for almost all practical
purposes. Whether a win is possible with a single pawn usually depends
on whether the weaker side's king can establish a blockade. When the
defending king is in front of the pawn, and cannot be driven away, the
game is completely drawn. See Diagram 119.

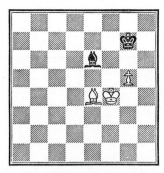

119. *Black to play*

Black keeps his king where it is, moves his bishop around, and White can make no progress.

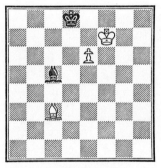

120. *White to play*

When the stronger side controls the queening square, his winning prospects are much brighter. In this example (Diagram 120) White can manoeuvre to stop Black's bishop sacrificing itself for the pawn: **1 B—B6 ch, K—B1.** If 1...K—B2, then 2 B—K7, B—B7; 3 B—Q6 ch!. **2 B—K7, B—B7; 3 B—Q6, B—R5; 4 B—K5,** and White wins, as Black has no defence against the threatened 5 B—B6 and 6 P—K7.

Same-coloured bishop endgames, with two pawns against one, can often be won by sacrificing a pawn so as to capture

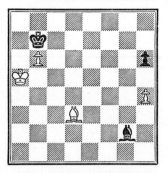

121. Eliskases *v* Capablanca
(*Semmering-Baden*, 1937)
White to play

the defender's only pawn and reach a winning king and pawn endgame. But this example (Diagram 121) shows both the drawing influence of a RP, and that even Capablanca, the greatest endgame player of all time, could mishandle a simple ending.

1 B—R6 ch   K—N1!

The only move to draw. Capablanca blundered by 1...K—B3?, and lost after 2 B—B8, B—B8; 3 B—N4, and some subtle and clever tempo play by White.

2 K—N4   B—N2!
3 B×B

If 3 B—K2, B—N7; 4 K—B5, then 4...K—N2!, and Black's king cannot be driven from this blockading square.

3 ...   K×B
4 K—B5   P—R4

with a clear draw. White's king will win the RP, but Black's king will reach KR1.

Diagram 122 makes a more complex endgame with bishops of same colour, in which Spassky's advantage consists of space and squares rather than material. Five of Black's seven pawns are on squares of the same colour as his own bishop, while only one of White's pawns is similarly restrictive. White's advanced pawn at QR6 is a focal point for queening combinations

1 P—B4!   P×P

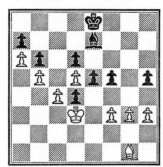

122. Spassky v R. Byrne
(6th game, Candidates', 1974)
White to play

Giving up a pawn to try to keep the position blocked. If 1...B—B3, White has the typical break-through 2 P×P, P×P; 3 P—B5!, P×P; 4 P—N6!, and wins. 1...K—Q2 might be tried, although 2 P—B5, still looks strong.

2	P×P		K—Q2
3	B×P		K—B2
4	B—B3		K—Q2
5	B—N4		K—B2
6	K—K3		B—B3
7	K—B3		P—R5

Another pawn goes on to a dark square; but White was threatening 8 K—N3, followed by B—B3—N7—R6—N5, and finally K—R4, picking up the KRP.

8	K—K3		B—N2
9	K—Q3		B—B3
10	B—Q2		K—B1
11	B—K3		K—B2
12	B—B2		

Zugzwang! The black bishop has to stay at KB3, else he either loses the KRP or permits the winning manoeuvre B—Q4—N7—R6—N5. The king cannot go to Q1 or Q2 because of 13 B×P ch, P×B; 14 P—R7. So ...

12 ...   K—B1

123. *White to play*

13 P—B5!

The winning idea, which exploits both the black pawns on dark squares and the queening possibilities of White's QRP.

13	...		QP×P
14	P—Q6		K—Q2
15	B×BP		B—Q1

If 15...P×B, then 16 P—N6, and wins.

16	B—N4		K—K3
17	K—B4		B—B3
18	B—B5		B—Q1
19	B—Q4!		K×P
20	B—K5 ch		K—K3
21	B—N8		K—Q2
22	K—Q5		Resigns

The finish could be 22...B—B3; 23 B×P, K—B2 (trying to keep the bishop out of play); 24 K—K6, B—Q5; 25 K×P, followed by K—N6, and the advance of the KBP.

Bishops of Opposite Colours

Pawn blockade is the key defensive manoeuvre in endgames with bishops of opposite colour. If the weaker side can blockade the pawns, he can generally draw; otherwise the player with the material advantage has chances to win. Fine's well-known reference work *Basic Chess Endings* states that the endgame of bishop and two disconnected passed pawns versus bishop of opposite colour is won if the pawns are separated by two or more empty files. Even grandmasters quote Fine's rule, but it is far from automatic – it all depends on the position of the kings, bishops, and pawns. See Diagram 124.

124. N. Miller *v* Saidy
(American Open, 1971)
White to play

125. Bernstein *v* Mednis
(U.S. Championship, 1961–62)
Black to play

Both sides knew Fine's 'rule', and White resigned. Saidy writes in *Chess Life and Review* that 'the next morning, bleary-eyed (these weekend marathons are sheer masochism) I was pounced upon by Walter Browne and Norman Lessing, who claimed that the final position (see Diagram 124) was drawn! Incredible, didn't they know BCE? I bet them hard cash that it was won. After a half hour of analysis I forked over the dough – they were right!'

The reason for the draw in Diagram 124 is that White's king and bishop have set up an unbreakable blockade. The difference in the position of the two kings is the key. White's is active, and prevents the black king from wandering down the board in support of the pawns.

and White now resigned in view of the probable finish: 5...B—N2; 6 B—K8, B—R3; 7 K—Q1, K—Q6; 8 B—R4, B—N2; 9 B—N5 ch, K—K6; 10 B—K8, P—B5; 11 B×P, K—B7; 12 B—K4, P—B6; 13 P—R5, K—K6; 14 B—B6, P—KB7; 15 B—N2, K—B5, followed by ...K—N6—R7—N8 winning.

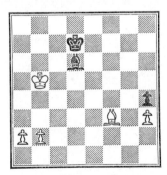

126. Walther *v* Fischer
(*Zurich*, 1959)
White to play

At first sight, the position in Diagram 125 is similar to Diagram 124, but the vital difference, that Black's king is active, means that Black can cash in his two pawns advantage despite the opposite colour bishop. Black won by 1...K—B3; 2 K—B3, K—K4; 3 K—K2, P—B4; 4 P—R4, K—K5; 5 B—R4,

White had a great chance in Diagram

126 for an upset victory, but he neglected the principle that the weaker side, in endgames with bishops of opposite colours, should not be given a chance to blockade the pawns.

1 P—R4?

The correct winning idea is: 1 P—N4!, K—B2; 2 K—R5!, K—N1; 3 P—N5, B—R6; 4 P—N6, K—B1; 5 K—R6, K—N1; 6 B—K4, B—B4; 7 P—R4, B—Q5; 8 P—R5, B—B6; 9 K—N5, followed by 10 P—R6, and 11 P—R7.

1 . . .   K—B2
2 P—N4   K—N1
3 P—R5   K—R2

Now there is no win because of the blockade. After **4 K—B4, B—N6; 5 K—N3, B—K8; 6 K—R4, B—Q7; 7 B—R5, B—K8; 8 P—N5, B—B7; 9 B—K2, B—K6; 10 K—N3, B—Q7; 11 P—N6 ch, K—N2; 12 K—R4, K—B3; 13 B—N5 ch, K—B4; 14 B—K8, B—K8**, a **draw** was agreed. After **15 P—N7, B—N6; 16 P—R6, K—N3**, White's pawns can make no further progress.

Endgames of bishop against knight without rooks

In endgames of bishop against knight without rooks, a key factor is the bishop's mobility. If there are pawns on both sides of the board, and more particularly if there is an outside passed pawn, or a wing majority, the player with the bishop has good winning chances. But if the player with the bishop has his pawns blocked on the 'wrong' colour – the same colour as his bishop – then the knight has the advantage. If the pawns are on one side of the board only, or spread over four files or fewer, this also is to the advantage of the knight. In these last two instances, the bishop's range and mobility is restricted, while the knight will have targets for attack and can benefit from its ability to control squares of either colour. In the majority of practical instances, a bishop versus knight endgame favours the bishop.

127. Spassky *v* Fischer
(*Santa Monica*, 1966)
White to play

See Diagram 127 for a typical case favouring the bishop, because of the pawns on both sides of the board. Spassky sums up the endgame in a comment in the tournament book: 'White has a pawn plus on the king side, and the superiority of a bishop over a knight, plus the facts that all the black pawns are isolated and that the white king has the possibility of moving to the black king side. All this speaks for the clear positional superiority of White.'

1 P—KR4

Fixing Black's pawn on the same colour as the bishop, and so restraining the mobility of Fischer's king.

1 . . .	N—B5
2 K—K2	N—K4

If 2...N—Q3, then 3 K—Q3, N—B4?; 4 P—R5.

3 K—K3	K—B3
4 K—B4	N—B2
5 K—K3	P—N4

Better 5...N—Q3, not allowing White a passed pawn.

6 P—R5	N—R3

Again N—Q3 is better, though White would still win by marching his king to the QR file. As played, the win is easy, since Black's knight is tied to watching the passed pawn.

7 K—Q3	K—K4
8 B—R8	K—Q3
9 K—B4	P—N5
10 P—R4	N—N1
11 P—R5	N—R3
12 B—K4	P—N6
13 K—N5	N—N1
14 B—N1	N—R3
15 K—R6	K—B3
16 B—R2	Resigns

There is no defence, for instance 16...K—B2; 17 K×P, K—B3; 18 B—B4 (threat K—N8), K—B2; 19 B—Q5, followed by K—R6—N5.

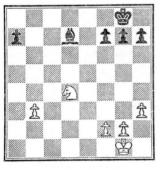

128. Stoltz v Kashdan
(The Hague, 1928)
Black to play

Here, in Diagram 128, the pawns are evenly balanced, but there are enough pawns for the bishop's mobility to be felt, and too few for the knight to have any chances of a blockade. The winning process is for Black to centralize his king, and to use his superior mobility to attack the white pawns on one or other flank.

1 . . .	K—B1
2 K—B1	K—K2
3 K—K2	K—Q3
4 K—Q3	K—Q4
5 P—R4	B—B1
6 N—B3	B—R3 ch
7 K—B3	

If 7 K—K3, K—B4; 8 N—N5, K—N5, when the penetration on the queen's side wins the QNP, and will force White to give up his knight.

7 . . .	P—R3
8 N—Q4	P—N3
9 N—B2	K—K5

Now the king is ready to march in for a meal of the king's-side pawns; but first the black pawns are advanced in support, so as to bring them nearer queening.

10 N—K3	P—B4
11 K—Q2	P—B5
12 N—N4	P—R4
13 N—B6 ch	K—B4
14 N—Q7	

Or 14 N—Q5, B—N2; 15 N—K7 ch, K—B3; 16 N—N8 ch, K—B2; 17 N—R6 ch, K—N2, and wins.

14 . . .	B—B1
15 N—B8	P—N4
16 P—N3	P×RP
17 P×RP	K—N5

The king and bishop have successfully combined to prevent the white knight getting counterplay; and now Black is ready to capture the KRP, and queen his own KRP.

18 N—N6	B—B4
19 N—K7	B—K3
20 P—N4	K×P

21 K—Q3	K—N5
22 K—K4	P—R5
23 N—B6	B—B4 ch
24 K—Q5	P—B6!

Stopping White's last hope of N—K5 ch, followed by N—B3.

25 P—N5	P—R6
26 N×P	P—R7
27 P—N6	P—R8=Q
28 N—B6	Q—QN8
29 K—B5	B—K5
30 Resigns	

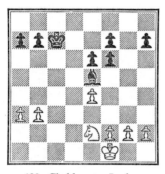

129. Chekhover *v* Lasker
(*Moscow*, 1935)
Black to play

The superiority of the bishop over the knight is fairly slight in Diagram 129, but is enhanced by two other factors: Black's king is better placed, while White's queen's-side pawns are vulnerable. The pawn at QR3 can be attacked by the bishop, and if it advances to QR4, then the QN4 square can be invaded by the black king. Lasker won by 1...P—N4; 2 K—K1, B—N7; 3 P—QR4, P×P; 4 P×P, K—B3; 5 K—Q2, K—B4; 6 N—B3, K—N5; 7 N—N5, P—QR4; 8 N—Q6, K×P; 9 K—B2, B—K4; 10 N×P, B×P; 11 N—Q8, P—K4; 12 N—B6, B—N8; 13 P—B3, B—B4; 14 N—N8, K—N4; 15 P—N4, B—K2; 16 P—N5, P×P; 17 N—Q7, B—Q3; 18 N—B6, K—B5; 19 Resigns, for if 19 N×P, then B—K2 traps the knight. Although a RP normally reduces the stronger side's winning chances in an endgame, the reverse is the case here where the RP, the bishop controlling its queening square, and the king in support, combine to prevent the knight setting up a blockade.

130. Averbakh *v* Lilienthal
(*Moscow*, 1949)
White to play

The knight has an obvious advantage in Diagram 130. Not only is it securely established on an ideal blockade square at Q4, but Black's bishop is handicapped with four pawns on light squares. White wins by first ensuring that Black's light-square pawn formation is permanently fixed, then invading with king or knight:
1 P—N5, P×P. If 1...P—B4; 2 N—B3, B—K1; 3 N—K5, K—Q1; 4 K—B3, K—K2; 5 K—K3, K—K3; 6 K—K5, P—R4; 9 N—Q3, K—K2; 7 N—Q3, K—K3; 8 N—K5, P—R4; 9 N—Q3, B—Q2; 10 P—R4, B—K1; 11 P—N4, and the passed pawn is decisive.
2 P×P, B—B1; 3 K—B4, P—R4; 4 K—K5, B—R3. Also after 4...B—N5, White's king forces its way towards Black's QBP: 5 K—B6, B—R4; 6 N—K6 ch, K—Q2; 7 N—B4, K—K1 (if 7...K—Q1; 8 N×B, P×N; 9 P—N6); 8 K—K6 (not N×B?, P×N; 9 K—B5, K—B2, when Black catches his opponent in the trébuchet and wins), B—B6; 9 K—Q6, and White's king invasion proves decisive.
5 K—B6, B—Q6; 6 K—K7, B—N8; 7 P—R3, B—K5; 8 N—K6 ch, K—N2; 9

K—Q6, B—B7; 10 N—Q4, B—Q8; 11 N×P, and White wins.

K—R2. Virtual resignation, but if 11 K—B2, N×QP ch; or if 11 K—B1, K—Q7; 12 K—N1, K—K8; 13 K—R2, K—B7, and wins. 11...K—Q7; 12 P—N3, N×QP; 13 B×P, K—K6; 14 P×P, P×P; 15 Resigns. If 15 K—N2, N—K8 ch; or 15 B—N4, N—K8, winning.

131. Lehmann *v* Fuderer
(*Munich*, 1954)
Black to play

Note that in Diagram 131 all White's pawns are on the same coloured squares as his bishop. They are spread over only five files and both Black's king and knight have entry points into the enemy position via the dark squares – so Black has good winning chances.
1...N—K7. Stopping White's king from joining in the game by K—N1. 2 B—B4, P—R5; 3 K—R2, N—B5?. Black plays inaccurately here. He should continue 3...K—K2, intending to bring the king to K6, and, if necessary to advance the KBP to KB5 before launching the final attack against the QP.
4 K—N1?. Instead, 4 P—N3 would make it much harder for Black. 4...K—K2. Now everything runs smoothly again. 5 B—N5, K—Q3; 6 B—K8, P—B3; 7 B—N5, K—B4; 8 B—B4, K—Q5; 9 K—B1, K—B6; 10 K—N1, K—B7; 11

132. Levenfish *v* Ragosin
(*Leningrad-Moscow*, 1939)
White to play

In Diagram 132, White has a passed pawn, and this is the key factor. White wins by using the pawn as a decoy, to enable his king and knight to eat the black pawns on the other flank:
1 N—Q2, K—K1; 2 K—B3, B—K2; 3 P—B6, K—Q1. If 3...P—B4; 4 P×P, P×P; 5 N—B4, B—B3; 6 N—Q6 ch, K—Q1; 7 P—B7 ch wins. 4 K—K4, K—B2; 5 K—Q5, P—B4; 6 P×P, P×P; 7 K×P, K×P; 8 N—N3, B—Q3 ch; 9 K—K6, B—R7; 10 N—Q4 ch, K—B4; 11 N×P, P—R4; 12 N—N3, K—Q5; 13 K—B5, P—R5; 14 N—R5, B—N8; 15 P—B3, B—B7; 16 N—B4, B—K8; 17 N—N6, K—Q4; 18 K—N4, and wins.

Queen endgames

The reputation of queen endgames for being exceptionally difficult is in some respects exaggerated. When one player has a strong passed pawn or a centralized king and queen, while his opponent's pieces are immobile, then queen endings can be as straightforward to win as a simple knight versus bad bishop endgame. The difficulties occur when a passed pawn cannot easily be created, or when the superior side's king is exposed to threats of perpetual check.

133. Botvinnik *v* Donner
(*Noordwijk*, 1965)
Black to play

Black has a difficult position in Diagram 133. The passed pawn White creates by force on the queen's side is more mobile than the black RP, while White's queen is very mobile compared with Black's, which is hindered by the three KBPs. 1...Q—N3, loses to 2 Q—K4!

1 . . .   K—N1

The king has to get as close as possible to QR1.

2 P—R4   Q—R8 ch
3 K—K2   P—R4
4 Q—Q5 ch   K—R2

4...K—B1 is dubious, because of the threats of the white QRP reaching QR8 with check.

5 Q—Q1!   Q—R7?

The queen is badly placed here; any other queen retreat would be better.

6 P—N4   P—R5
7 Q—KB1!

Now 7...P—R6; 8 P—R5, P×P; 9 P×P, Q—N7; 10 P—R6, leads to the loss of Black's RP.

7 . . .   P—N4
8 P—R5   P×P
9 P×P   P—N5
10 P—R6   Resigns

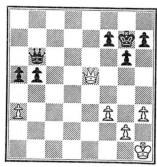

134. D. M. Williams *v* N. R. Benjamin
(Under-14 championship, *London*, 1974)
Black to play

Black is a pawn up, and the 2–1 queen's-side majority means he has a potential passed pawn. The first stage of the winning process – to establish the passed pawn and get the queen backing it – is comparatively simple. But White counters in the best way by loosening the pawns in front of the black king, so as to improve the chances of perpetual check. Black then has the more difficult task of evading the threat of continuous checks, which he does through a king march down the board from KN3 to Q7. The player of Black was only 13 at the time of the game, and won a special prize for his mature and confident handling of this advanced ending.
   1...Q—B3!. After 1...P—B3; 2 Q—K7 ch, or 1...K—R3; 2 Q—B4 ch, White would have good chances of

perpetual check. 2 Q×P, Q—R8 ch; 3 K—R2, Q×P; 4 Q—K5 ch, K—N1; 5 Q—K8 ch, Q—B1; 6 Q—N5, Q—R1; 7 Q—R4, Q—R2; 8 Q—K8 ch, K—N2; 9 Q—K5 ch, P—B3; 10 Q—R1, P—R5; 11 Q—R3, Q—Q2; 12 K—N3, K—B2; 13 Q—R2 ch, K—K2; 14 Q—K2 ch, Q—K3; 15 Q—KB2, Q—Q3 ch; 16 P—B4, P—R6; 17 Q—K3 ch, K—B1; 18 Q—R7, P—N4; 19 Q—R8 ch, K—N2; 20 Q—R7 ch, K—N3; 21 K—R2, Q×P ch; 22 K—N1, Q—B8 ch; 23 K—R2, Q—N7; 24 Q—R8, Q—N6; 25 Q—K8 ch, Q—B2; 26 Q—K4 ch, K—N2; 27 Q—R8, P—R7; 28 K—R1, Q—K3; 29 Q—R7 ch, K—N3; 30 Q—R5, Q—N6; 31 Q—R8, Q—N8 ch; 32 K—R2, P—R8=Q; 33 Q—K8 ch, K—B4!. Starting the king march which escapes the queen checks. 34 Q—Q7 ch, K—B5; 35 P—N3 ch, K—B6; 36 Q—Q5 ch, K—K6; 37 Q—B5 ch, K—Q7; 38 Q—Q5 ch, Q—Q6; 39 Resigns.

while the white king does the marching. The white king's aim is to reach the same rank as the black king, or else stand close to it, so as to reduce Black's available checks, and eventually force a queen swap by interposing his own queen with check.

1 Q—B6!, the only way. 1 K—R6, Q—R5 ch; 2 K—N7, Q—R6 would make the win harder. The white king stands badly at the far end of the board (sixth, seventh and eighth ranks), because this leaves the black queen with too much freedom. 1...Q—Q4 ch; 2 Q—B5, Q—Q1 ch; 3 K—R5, Q—K1. After 3...Q—R1 ch; 4 K—N4, Q—N2, White makes progress by 5 Q—B7, Q—B6; 6 P—N7. 4 Q—B4 ch, K—R4; 5 Q—Q2 ch, K—R5; 6 Q—Q4 ch, K—R4; 7 K—N5, Q—K2 ch; 8 K—B5, Q—B1 ch; 9 K—K4. Once again the checks have come to an end, and the white king is well placed in the centre.

9...Q—R3; 10 Q—K5 ch, K—R5; 11 P—N7, Q—R8 ch; 12 K—Q4, Q—Q8 ch; 13 K—B5, Q—B8 ch; 14 K—Q6, Q—Q7 ch. Or 14...Q—R6 ch; 15 K—Q5. 15 K—K6, Q—R7 ch; 16 Q—Q5, Q—K7 ch; 17 K—Q6, Q—R7 ch; 18 K—B5!, Resigns. The final position in this endgame shows the winning method with great clarity.

135. Botvinnik v Minev
(*Amsterdam*, 1954)
White to play

Diagram 135 shows the concluding stages of a notable endgame where Botvinnik upset the existing textbook verdict that a queen and NP against a queen should be a draw. Up till this game, players and analysts had tried unsuccessfully to win, by using the king to protect the pawn, and roaming the board with the queen. In fact, as Botvinnik shows, the queen should shepherd the pawn from a central square

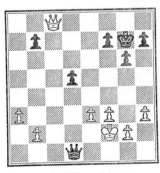

136. Alekhine v Maroczy
(*New York*, 1924)
Black to play

One danger which the stronger side has to guard against in a queen and

pawn endgame, is a snap perpetual check. In Diagram 136, even the great Alekhine neglected this precaution: 1 Q×P?, Instead, 1 Q—B3 ch, K—N1; 2 Q—Q4, centralizing the queen, would win for White. 1...Q—Q7 ch; 2 K—N3, P—Q5!; 3 P×P. Otherwise Black would get a dangerous passed pawn. 3...Q—N4 ch, and Black keeps checking along the diagonal KN4 to QB8, for perpetual check.

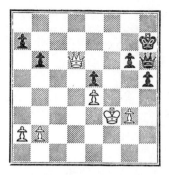

138. Alexander *v* Reshevsky
(*Nottingham*, 1936)
Black to play

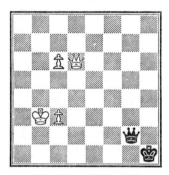

137. Bilek *v* Heidenfeld
(*Lugano*, 1968)
Black to play

Black had played a difficult queen endgame a few months before, so knew the traps inherent in this type of position (Diagram 137). White is winning, but failed to observe that Black has moved his king to KR8 to set up a potential stalemate. The game concluded **1...Q—N1 ch; 2 P—B4??.** White's extra pawns would win after 2 K—N4. **2...Q—N6 ch!; 3 Q×Q, drawn by stalemate.**

continual threats to White's KP; (*d*) having thus reduced White to passivity, he is ready for combined action by his king, queen, and KNP. All this is easier said than done!

1 . . .	Q—N4!
2 Q—K6	

If 2 Q—B7 ch, K—R3; 3 Q×RP, Q—N5 ch; 4 K—B2, P—R5; 5 P×P, Q×P ch; 6 K—K3, Q—B5 ch, and Black will win the KP with check.

2 . . .	K—R3
3 Q—B8	Q—B3 ch
4 K—N2	P—R5!

Thus Black creates the passed pawn which he needs in order to make real progress.

5 P×P	K—R4
6 Q—Q7	P—R4
7 Q—Q1 ch	K×P
8 Q—K1 ch	K—R4
9 Q—Q1 ch	K—R3
10 Q—R1 ch	K—N4
11 Q—Q1	K—R3
12 Q—R1 ch	K—N2
13 Q—QB1	Q—Q1
14 Q—B2	Q—N4 ch

Diagram 138 is an example of a more complex queen endgame, in which high technical skill is required to cash in Black's extra pawn. The ending can be logically divided into the following stages: (*a*) Black plays ...P—R5, creating a passed KNP; (*b*) he guards the queen's-side pawns from attack; (*c*) he combines this defensive policy with

Whereas White's checks achieve nothing, Black greatly improves his position by finally getting his queen to KB7, where it is well placed to support the further advance of the KNP.

15 K—R3	Q—K6 ch
16 K—N4	Q—B5 ch
17 K—R3	Q—B6 ch
18 K—R2	

If 18 K—R4, then 18...K—R3; 19 Q—Q2 ch, Q—B5 ch and wins.

18 . . .	K—R3
19 Q—B6	Q—B7 ch
20 K—R3	K—R4!

Better than 20.. Q×P; 21 Q—B6, with drawing chances for White. As played, White is reduced to two losing possibilities: (a) either he employs his queen to threaten the queen's-side pawns, when Black's king and KNP can advance; or (b) he keeps his queen at home, when Black's queen's-side pawns are in no danger, and Black can gradually make progress on the other flank. See Diagram 139.

21 Q—N7	Q—K6 ch
22 K—N2	Q—Q7 ch
23 K—N3	Q—Q6 ch
24 K—B2	Q—Q3!
25 K—N3	K—N4

Black's queen retreat was to guard

139. White to play

against Q—K7 ch at this point. The queen will soon force a new and decisive entry.

26 K—B3	Q—Q1
27 K—N3	Q—B3
28 Q—Q5	Q—B5 ch
29 K—N2	K—R5
30 Q—B6	Q—N6 ch
31 K—B1	Q—B6 ch
32 K—K1	Q—K6 ch
33 K—B1	P—KN4
34 K—N2	Q—Q7 ch
35 Resigns	

If 35 K—B3, P—N5 mate; or if 35 K—B1, K—N6, and he must exchange queens.

7

FISCHER'S ENDGAME

In several games of his 1971 Candidates' matches Robert Fischer showed superb technique in the handling of rook and bishop versus rook and knight endgames. These endgames represent an important addition to chess knowledge, as they give many useful pointers to the way that such endings should be handled. This is especially valuable since this ending is scarcely dealt with in books on the endgame; for example Reuben Fine in *Basic Chess Endings* does not give a single position of this type. Fine, like other authors of endgame books, simply states that endings of this type are no more than simple addition of the parts, but many players have found, often to their cost, that, even if they study rook endings, bishop endings, and knight endings (and how many players can claim to have done that?), though they may be able to play these individual endings very well they, nonetheless, have difficulty in handling endgames of a composite nature. This and the following chapter on Petrosian's Endgame are designed to help fill this gap.

The principles to be learned from Fischer's endgame may be summed up as:
1. Activate one's own pieces – this applies equally here as it does in all endings.
2. Attempt to restrict the opponent's pieces (especially the knight).
3. Avoid situations in which the knight can be exchanged for the bishop to reach a drawn rook and pawn ending.
4. Use the bishop's superiority over the knight (this superiority is generally emphasized by the presence of the rooks) to force the defender to make concessions.
5. Stabilize the pawn chain so that the defender's pawns are vulnerable to attack by rook or bishop.
6. Infiltrate with the king – again this applies to this as all other endgames.
7. Maintain the initiative and keep the defender's chances of active counterplay to a minimum.
8. Offer to swap rooks in situations where the exchange will lead to a won bishop versus knight endgame.

140. Fischer *v* Taimanov
(4th game, Candidates', 1971)
White to play

1	B—B1	P—QR4
2	B—B4	

White's bishop has forced a weakening of Black's QN4 square and now Black's rook is tied to the defence of the KBP.

2	...	R—KB1
3	K—N2	

White's plan is gradually to strengthen his position. Black's pieces have been tied down and cannot easily become active. White will fix the queen's-side pawns by P—QR4, retaining QN5 and QB4 for his piece manoeuvres and king penetration Then the advance of the king's-side pawns will provoke new weaknesses.

3	...	K—Q3
4	K—B3	N—Q2
5	R—K3	N—N1

Taimanov is trying to find a good square for his knight, but Fischer has seen to it that there is none available.

6	R—Q3 ch	K—B2
7	P—B3	N—B3
8	R—K3	K—Q3
9	P—QR4	

See Diagram 141.

Black's queen's side has been weakened and now it is fixed, but how is White to strengthen his position still further? Fischer's next moves show three of the basic themes of his endgame:

141. *Black to play*

1. Several black pawns are fixed on the same colour complex as White's bishop (moves 11, 13, 16).
2. White keeps a grip on the queen and king files along which Black's rook might otherwise develop counterplay (moves 12–18).
3. White offers the exchange of rooks at the stage when his adjournment analysis (an important precision factor in the Fischer endgame) shows that he has a forced win (move 19).

9	...	N—K2
10	P—R3	N—B3
11	P—R4	P—R4

Black holds up the threatened advance P—R5, followed by P—KN4, K—N3—R4, P—N5, etc., when the pressure on Black's position would be intolerable. However, Black's defence involves the serious drawback of playing his pawns on to the same colour squares as the opposing bishop.

12	R—Q3 ch	K—B2
13	R—Q5	P—B4

This leaves Black's K3 square weak, but 13...P—N3, is met by 14 B—N5, preparing P—B5.

14	R—Q2	R—B3
15	R—K2	K—Q2

Keeping the rook out.

| 16 | R—K3 | P—N3 |

See Diagram 142.

All three of Black's pawns are now on light squares and are thus potential targets for the bishop; this cannot turn out well.

'Adjournment analysis showed that

142. *White to play*

White had a 20 move long winning manoeuvre. This was exactly what Fischer played' – Kotov.

17 B—N5	R—Q3
18 K—K2	

The immediate 18 R—Q3 only draws.

18 . . .	K—Q1

Black should avoid the exchange of rooks, but 18...K—B2, allowing White's rook to penetrate by 19 R—K8, would be a most unpleasant decision to make, and 18...R—B3 lets White's king come through via Q3 and QB4.

19 R—Q3!	K—B2
20 R × R	K × R
21 K—Q3	

Already threatening to exchange into a winning king and pawn ending.

21 . . .	N—K2
22 B—K8	

The beginning of a very instructive bishop manoeuvre There is one position which is lost for Black, because of zugzwang. Fischer attains this position after fourteen forced moves.

22 . . .	K—Q4

White's task is to get to QR6 with his king. Then he puts his bishop on K8, forcing ...K—Q1, and there follows the winning sacrifice of bishop for three pawns. It is important in this variation for the white pawns to remain on QN2 and QB3.

23 B—B7 ch	K—Q3
24 K—B4	K—B3
25 B—K8 ch	K—N2
26 K—N5	N—B1

The last part of the plan is difficult to realize, as Black has the piquant threat of ...N—Q3 mate.

27 B—B6 ch	

As soon as Black's king goes to Q4, B3 or N2. White checks it back, and White's king penetrates deeper and deeper into Black's position.

27 . . .	K—B2
28 B—Q5	N—K2
29 B—B7	

29 B—B3 and 29 B—N3 would only draw.

29 . . .	K—N2

White now manoeuvres his bishop to the long diagonal since otherwise his king gets no further – Fischer shows how it is done.

30 B—N3	K—R2

If 30...N—B1, then 31 B—Q5 ch, and the white king enters at QR6 or QB6.

31 B—Q1	K—N2
32 B—B3 ch	K—B2

If 32...K—R2, then 33 P—B4!, and 35 K—B6, followed by a king march to the king's-side pawns.

33 K—R6	

Second part of the plan completed.

33 . . .	N—N1
34 B—Q5	N—K2

Nor is 34...N—B3 of any use: 35 B—B7, N—K5; 36 B × P, N × NP; 37 P—B4, K—B3; 38 K—R7, K—B2; 39 B—B7, N—K7; 40 B × P, N × P; 41 B—B7, and the advance of the KRP is decisive.

35 B—B4	N—B3
36 B—B7	

Now that White's king has arrived at R6, the bishop goes to attack the pawn again.

36 . . .	N—K2
37 B—K8	

143. *Black to play*

The required position is achieved, see Diagram 143. Black is in zugzwang.

37 . . .   K—Q1
38 B×P!

Converting his positional advantage into a solid front of passed pawns.

38 . . .   N×B
39 K×P   K—Q2

If 39...N—K2, then the QRP goes.

40 K×BP   N—K2
41 P—QN4   P×P
42 P×P

Two united passed pawns and an active king are good enough to win. The game concluded: 42...N—B1; 43 P—R5, N—Q3; 44 P—N5, N—K5 ch; 45 K—N6, K—B1; 46 K—B6, K—N1; 47 P—N6, Black resigns.

In Diagram 144 Fischer has already won a pawn and forced Black's knight out of play. The rest is a matter of simple technique: 1 B—Q4, P—B6; 2 B—K3, P—R3; 3 P×P, N—B3; 4 R—Q6, K—B2; 5 R×N ch, K×R; 6 B—Q4 ch, K—N4; 7 P—R7, K—B5; 8 K—R2, P—N4; 9 P—R8=Q, R×Q ch; 10 B×R, P—N5; 11 P—K5, Black resigns.

The win here was very simple, but the ending is interesting from a historical point of view, as it appears to be the first example in Fischer's career of the 'Fischer endgame'.

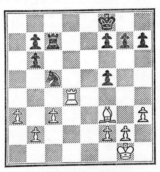

145. Fischer *v* Barcza
(Interzonal, *Stockholm*, 1962)
White to play

From Diagram 145 play went: **1 R—QN4**, N—Q2; **2 K—B1**, K—K2; **3 K—K2**, K—Q1; **4 R—N5**, P—N3; **5 K—K3**, K—B1. Black can now free his rook from the defence of the QNP, but meanwhile White has been able to centralize his king. **6 K—Q4**, K—N1; **7 K—Q5**, R—B3; **8 K—Q4**, R—R3; **9 P—QR4**, K—B2; **10 P—R5**. Played to open a line of attack against Black's weak pawn on QN2. **10...R—Q3 ch; 11 B—Q5**, K—B1; **12 P×P**, P—B3. If 12...N×P, then 13 K—K5. **13 K—K3**, N×P; **14 B—N8**, K—B2. 14...P—R3 is met by 15 B—R7, and 14...P—R4, by B—B7.

15 R—B5 ch, K—N1; **16 B×P**, N—Q4 ch; **17 K—B3**, N—K2; **18 P—R4!**. Threatening to smash Black's already weakened king's-side pawns by 19 P—

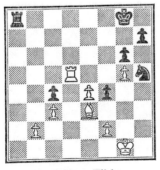

144. Fischer *v* Eliskases
(*Mar del Plata*, 1960)
White to play

R5. **18...P—N3; 19 R—N5, K—N2; 20 P—R5, K—R3; 21 P—B4, P×P; 22 B×P, R—Q5; 23 P—QN3, N—B3.** Black also loses after 23...N×B; 24 R×N, R—Q6 ch; 25 K—K4, R×P; 26 R×BP.

24 K—K3, R—Q1; 25 B—K4, N—R4; 26 B—B2, P—R5; 27 R—R5, R—K1 ch; 28 K—Q2, R—KN1; 29 R×P, P—N4. Or 29...R×P; 30 R—B4. **30 R—B4, P×P; 31 P×P, R×P; 32 R×P ch, K—R2; 33 K—B3, R—N5; 34 P—B4, N—N2; 35 K—N4, Black resigns.**

In connection with the above game it is interesting to note an observation made by Keres in *The Games of Robert J. Fischer:* 'He made a big step forward in endgame technique (in the Stockholm Interzonal). His endgame wins against Portisch and Barcza being excellent examples of exploiting small advantages.'

6 B—K5, N—Q4. Not 6...N×P?; 7 R×R ch, P×R; 8 B×P, P—B4; 9 K—B4, P—B5; 10 K×P, P—B6; 11 P—N4!, P—B7; 12 B—N2, P×P; 13 P—R5, and White wins.

7 R—Q1!, N—B3?. Tal should have given back the pawn, in order to centralize his forces, with 7...R—B4; 8 B×P, K—Q2. **8 K—B4, P—KN3; 9 P—B3!.** An intermediate phase – Fischer ensures that Black's pieces will remain passive before attempting stage two – the infiltration of Black's weakened king's side.

9...N—Q2; 10 B—Q6, R—B7; 11 P—N3!, R—K7. 11...R×P, fails to 12 R—K1, K—Q1; 13 R—K6, and then 14 R×NP. **12 K—N5, R—K3; 13 B—B4, N—B1; 14 R—Q6, P—R4; 15 K—R6, R—K7; 16 R—Q2, R—K2.**

147. *White to play*

White has made great progress in the invasion of the king's side. Now further weakening (stage three) is necessary, and then stage four will be a simple matter of mopping up.

17 B—Q6, R—R2 ch; 18 K—N5, R—KB2. 18...N—Q2 loses to the problem-like 19 K×P, R—R1; 20 K—N7, R—K1; 21 K—B7!. **19 R—QN2!.** Zugzwang. **19...P—B5; 20 B×P, R—B4 ch; 21 K—R6, P—QN4; 22 B—Q6, P—N5.** 22...R×P; loses material to 23 R×P, with the threat of 24 R—N8 ch. **23 P—N4, R×P; 24 P—N5, N—K3; 25 K×P, R—Q6; 26 B—K5, R—K6; 27 K—B5, N—B1; 28 R—N2, R—B6 ch; 29 B—B4, K—Q2; 30 P—N6, N—K3; 31 P—N7!.** Forcing a simple winning endgame.

31...R×B ch; 32 K—K5, R—B1; 33 P×R=Q, N×Q; 34 K—Q5, P—R5; 35 R—N7 ch, K—K1; 36 K—Q6, P—N6; 37 P—R3, Black resigns.

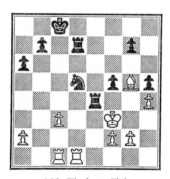

146. Fischer *v* Tal
(Candidates', *Curacao*, 1962)
White to play

Black's pieces are very active and well centralized in Diagram 146. The first stage of the ending is for White to activate his own forces: **1 R—Q3, R—QB5; 2 R(B1)—Q1!.** Fischer sacrifices a pawn to activate his pieces and eliminate a pair of rooks, bringing the position down to the Fischer endgame proper. **2...R×BP; 3 R×R ch, N×R; 4 R—QB1, R—QB2; 5 B—B4, R—B3;**

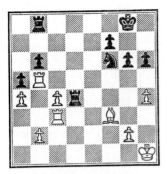

148. Fischer *v* Taimanov
(Interzonal, *Palma*, 1970)
White to play

In Diagram 148 Black had sealed the faulty ...R(Q2)—Q5?, whereas ...R (Q2)—Q1 would have retained drawing chances. Now Fischer was able, forcefully, to demonstrate the power of his endgame.
1 P—B5!, R×P ch; **2 K—N1**, R—QN5; **3 R×R!**. The only way to win. **3...P×R; 4 R—B4**, P×P. 4...N—Q2, allows White to obtain connected passed pawns by 5 P—B6, N—K4; 6 P—B7, N×B ch; 7 P×N, R—QB1; 8 K—B2, K—B1; 9 K—K3, K—K2; 10 R×P, with an assured win.
5 R×BP, K—N2; **6 P—R5**, R—K1; **7 R—B1**. Manoeuvring to get behind the passed pawn. **7...R—K4; 8 R—R1!**, R—K2; **9 K—B2!**. 9 P—R6, would allow 9...R—R2, followed by N—Q2—B4, with good drawing prospects. **9...N—K1; 10 P—R6**, R—R2; **11 K—K3**, N—B2; **12 B—N7**, N—K3; **13 R—R5**, K—B3; **14 K—Q3**, K—K2; **15 K—B4**, K—Q3; **16 R—Q5 ch**, K—B2; **17 K—N5!**, Black resigns.

In this position (Diagram 149) many players would be searching for ways of exchanging off all the pieces into a winning king and pawn endgame, but Fischer finds a more effective method of ending the game. **1...B—Q4!; 2 R—K8 ch**, K—N2; White resigns – he cannot save the knight.

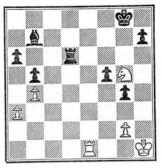

149. Larsen *v* Fischer
(6th game, Candidates', 1971)
Black to play

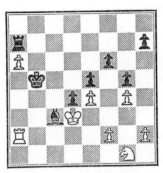

150. Petrosian *v* Fischer
(6th game, Candidates', 1971)
White to play

Black has a clear advantage in Diagram 150, as White's QRP is doomed. However, it cannot be taken at once, because White has an impregnable position in the ending of bishop versus knight. Black has first to play B—R4 which gives White time for countermeasures.

1 N—K2	B—R4
2 R—N2 ch	K×P
3 R—N1	R—QB2

Fischer has won the weak QRP, but in order to win the ending he must infiltrate with his rook.

4 R—N2

4 P—B3 would make it more difficult for Black to regroup his pieces.

4 . . .   B—K8!
5 P—B3

5 R—N1, B×P; 6 R—KB1, was suggested as a drawing line, but Black can instead retreat the bishop to R4 and try alternative winning plans, e.g. put his king on QB3, force White to put his rook on the QR file, and then march his king down the QN file.

5 . . .   K—R4!
6 R—B2   R—QN2
7 R—R2 ch   K—N4
8 R—N2 ch   B—N5
9 R—R2   R—QB2
10 R—R1   R—B1
11 R—R7?

After the correct 11 R—R2, B—K8; 12 R—N2 ch, K—R5; 13 R—B2!, Black would not find it easy to prove a win. Now, however, the white rook is cut off from his own camp.

11 . . .   B—R4
12 R—Q7

The KRP still cannot be captured: 12 R×P, B—N3; 13 R—KB7, R—QR1; 14 R×P, R—R6 ch; 15 K—Q2, B—R4 ch, and Black wins.

12 . . .   B—N3
13 R—Q5 ch   B—B4

Now the black rook can no longer be kept out, and the game ended: 14 N—B1, K—R5; 15 R—Q7, B—N5; 16 N—K2, K—N6; 17 R—QN7, R—QR1; 18 R×P. The rook ending 18 N—B1, K—N7; 19 R×B ch, K×N; is also lost. 18...R—R8; 19 N×P ch. Or 19 N—N3, R—R7; 20 N—B1, R—KB7. 19...P×N; 20 K×P, R—Q8 ch; 21 K—K3, B—B4 ch; 22 K—K2, R—KR8; 23 P—R4, K—B5; 24 P—R5, R—R7 ch; 25 K—K1, K—Q6; White resigns.

The sixth game had done nothing for Petrosian's confidence, and now, in the

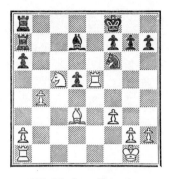

151. Fischer *v* Petrosian
(7th game, Candidates', 1971)
White to play

seventh, Fischer had achieved a big positional advantage (see Diagram 151), thanks to his queen's-side majority and, especially, his fine knight on QB5.

1 N×B ch!

As if to rub in his superiority, Fischer exchanges off his good knight (the immediate reason is that 1 P—QR4 – to prevent 1...B—N4 – would allow Black to set up some sort of defence with 1...B—B3, followed by...N—Q2), and forces a second consecutive win with the 'Fischer endgame'.

1 . . .   R×N
2 R—QB1

Threatening R—B6.

2 . . .   R—Q3
3 R—B7   N—Q2
4 R—K2

Already Black is lost – he has no good move (a knight move would allow R(2)—K7). The game concluded: 4... P—N3; 5 K—B2, P—KR4; 6 P—B4, P—R5; 7 K—B3, P—B4; 8 K—K3, P—Q5 ch; 9 K—Q2, N—N3; 10 R(2)—K7, N—Q4; 11 R—B7 ch, K—K1; 12 R—QN7, N×NP; 13 B—B4, Black resigns.

There is no answer to the threat of 14 R—KR7, R—KB3; 15 R—R8 ch, R—B1; 16 B—B7 ch, K—Q1; 17 R×R mate.

Anatoly Karpov

It is interesting to note that another grandmaster who has achieved important successes with Fischer's endgame is Anatoly Karpov. Karpov has been compared to Capablanca in his patient ability to build on small endgame advantages, and Fischer's endgame, with its theme of using the bishop's mobility to hem in the defender and deprive him of mobility, admirably suits Karpov's style. Here are three examples from his games:

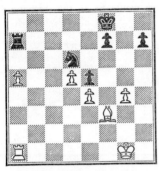

152. Karpov *v* Hübner
(Student Olympiad, *Graz*, 1972)
White to play

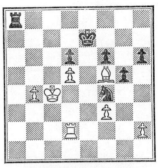

153. Karpov *v* Dueball
(Olympiad, *Skopje*, 1972)
Black to play

In Diagram 152 White is a clear pawn ahead, but his bishop is passively placed, and it appears that if White immediately advances his QRP, he cannot prevent Black from winning it.

1 P—R6	K—K2

The attempt to win the QRP with 1...N—N2, would rebound against Black after 2 B—K2, N—N4; 3 R—N1!, N×KP; 4 R—N7, R—R1; 5 P—R7, K—N2; 6 R—B7, when White would go on to win by the bishop manoeuvre B—N5—B6.

2 K—B2	K—Q2
3 K—K3	

The rest is simple technique: 3...N—B5 ch; 4 K—Q3, N—N3; 5 B—K2, K—Q3; 6 K—K3, N—Q2; 7 R—R1, N—B1; 8 R—R6 ch, K—K2; 9 P—Q6 ch, K—Q1; 10 B—N5, R—R1; 11 R—R5, P—B3; 12 R—R6, R—N1; 13 B—B6, R—N6 ch; 14 K—Q2, R—QR6; 15 R×BP, R—R7 ch; and Black resigns.

1 . . .	K—Q1
2 K—N5	K—B2

If 2...R—N1 ch, White can abandon the QNP in favour of direct attack, e.g. 3 K—B6, R×P; 4 K×P, R—N3 ch; 5 K—B5, R—N1; 6 R—R2, R—N2; 7 R—R8 ch, K—K2; 8 P—Q6 ch, and wins.

3 R—B2 ch	K—N2
4 B—Q7!	

4 R—B6? allows Black counterplay with 4...N—K7!

4 . . .	R—R6
5 R—B6!	R—Q6

If 5...N—K7; 6 B—B8 ch, K—N1; 7 K—N6 wins. 5...N×P; 6 R×P, N×P; 7 R×P!, or 5...R×P; 6 R—R6, N—Q6; 7 B—B6 ch, K—B2; 8 R—R7 ch, K—B1; 9 K—R5, N—K4; 10 P—N5 would also win for White in the long run.

6 R—N6 ch	K—B2
7 B—B6	N×P

8 **R—N7 ch**   **K—B1**

8...K—Q1 is no better, when 9 R—Q7 ch, K—B1; 10 R—KR7 wins.

9 **R—KB7**

This threatens 10 B×N, R×B ch; 11 K—B6, winning the rook, but 9 R—KR7!, would be even quicker, e.g. 9...N—B5; 10 R×P, P—B4; 11 R—B6, R—Q7; 12 R×BP, R×P; 13 R×P, with a clear win.

9 . . .   **K—Q1**
10 **R—Q7 ch**   **K—B1**
11 **R—KB7**   **K—Q1**
12 **K—B4**   **N—B5**

154. *White to play*

13 **R×P**

Not 13 P—N5, N—N3!, with good drawing chances after 14 K×R, N—K4 ch; 15 K—K4, N×R; 16 K—B5, K—K2; 17 P—N6, N—K4; 18 B—Q5, N—Q2; 19 P—N7, P—R4.

13 . . .   **P—Q4 ch**

If 13...K—B2, then 14 K—N5! wins, but not 14 R×N?, because R—R6! would draw.

14 **K—B5**   **K—K2**
15 **R×P**   **R—B6 ch**
16 **K—N6**   **R×P**
17 **P—N5**   **P—N5?**

After 17...R—K6, or even 17...R—QN6, White would still have winning chances, but now there is a clear win.

18 **R—R4!**   **R—KR6**
19 **R×P**   **N—K7**
20 **K—B7**

White could still go wrong with 20

B×P?, N—B6!, and Black would draw by sacrificing his knight for both the white pawns.

20 . . .   **R—R2**
21 **P—N6**   **K—K3 ch**
22 **K—Q8**   **N—Q5**
23 **R×N**   **K—Q3**
24 **B×P!**

This prevents the mate threat. Now Black would be on the receiving end: 24...R—R1 ch; 25 B—N8 ch, K—B3; 26 R—KN4, or 24...R×P; 25 P—N7, R—R1 ch; 26 B—N8 ch, K—B3; 27 P—N8=N ch!, K—N2; 28 R—N4 ch, K—R2; 29 K—B7, winning for White in both cases.

24 . . .   **K—B4**
25 **R—Q2**   **K×P**
26 **R—QB2**   **Resigns**

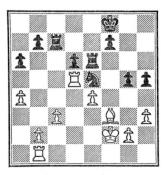

155. Karpov *v* Polugaevsky
(4th game, Candidates', 1974)
Black to play

This is an example of the Fischer endgame where, at the start of the ending, the bishop is rather inferior to the knight. When diagram 155 was reached seven moves before the adjournment, Karpov's trainer, grandmaster Furman, exclaimed 'Karpov and I will have a disturbed night! That terrible knight on Black's K4 won't let us sleep in peace.' But, due to Karpov's familiarity with the principles of the Fischer endgame, and Polugaevsky's failure to make the most of his chances, Black is completely outplayed in the endgame.

| 1 . . . | P—R5? |

Already an error. Better would be 1...R—KB3; threatening 2...P—N5.

| 2 R(N1)—Q1 | K—K2 |
| 3 R(Q1)—Q4 | P—B3? |

Another weak move, taking away a useful square from his own rook. Karpov now uses the Fischer endgame bishop to mobilize his pawn majority and advance it to where Black's rooks and knight are further immobilized.

4 P—R5	R—B3
5 B—K2	K—Q1
6 P—B4	K—B2
7 P—QN4	N—N3
8 P—N5	

The game was adjourned here, and it was clear that Karpov and Furman would be able to enjoy their beauty sleep.

| 8 . . . | P×P |
| 9 P×P | |

White recaptures away from the centre, so as to create a passed pawn on the distant QR file.

9 . . .	R—B7
10 P—N6 ch	K—Q2
11 R—Q2!	

Stifling Black's hope of active counterplay.

11 . . .	R×R
12 R×R	R—K4
13 P—R6	K—B3
14 R—N2	N—B5
15 P—R7	R—R4
16 B—B4	Resigns

For R—QR2 will decide.

___

This position (Diagram 156) shows that Boris Spassky also made use of the Fischer endgame technique.

156. Spassky v Benko
(Interzonal, *Amsterdam*, 1964)
White to play

1 B—B6	R—QR8
2 R×BP	R×P
3 B—R4	N—K5
4 R—B7?	

Spassky misses 4 R—B8 ch, K—R2; 5 R—B7, N—N6; 6 B—K8, with play on both sides of the board.

| 4 . . . | N—Q7? |

Black returns the compliment. 4... K—B1, to rob the bishop of the K8 square, is correct.

| 5 B—K8! | N×NP |

5...P—B3?; 6 B—N6, K—B1; 7 R—B7 ch, K—N1 (7...K—K1; 8 R× RP ch); 8 R—K7 is a straightforward win.

| 6 B×P ch | K—R2 |
| 7 P—R4 | |

The threat is 8 P—R5 and 9 B—N6 ch, with a mating net.

| 7 . . . | P—KR4 |
| 8 B×KP | N—Q5 |

The threat was 9 B—B5 ch, K—N1 (9...K—R3; 10 R—B6 ch); 10 B—N6!, etc.

| 9 B—Q5 | K—N3 |
| 10 R—Q7 | N—B4 |

Or 10...K—B3; 11 R—B7 ch, K—N3 (to save the KNP); 12 R—B4, with the threats 13 B—B7 ch, and 13 B—K4 ch, as well as 13 R×N.

11 P—B5	K—B3
12 P—B6	N—K2
13 P—B7	R—B6
14 B—N7	

Not 14 R—Q6 ch?, K—K4; 15 R—B6, R×R; 16 B×R, K—Q3!

14 . . .	P—R4
15 R×N	K×R
16 P—B8=Q	R×Q
17 B×R	P—R5
18 B—R6	Resigns

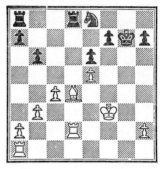

157. Petrosian *v* Portisch
(5th game, Candidates', 1974)
Black to play

Although Petrosian is the supreme exponent of the rook and knight against rook and bad bishop endgame, discussed in Chapter 8, he too has made use of the Fischer endgame, see Diagram 157. As in Diagram 155, the active bishop supports a queen's-flank majority, and in attempting to prevent an early defeat on the queen's side, Portisch fell into an attack on his king and knight:

1...P—B3. If 1...K—B1; 2 QR—Q1, K—K2; 3 P—B5, QR—N1; 4 P×P, P×P; 5 B×P, R×R; 6 B—B5 ch! and wins. **2 P×P ch, N×P; 3 R—KB1, K—R3; 4 R—K1, N—N1; 5 R×P ch, K—R4; 6 R—K5 ch, K—N3; 7 R—N2 ch, K—B2; 8 R—K4, N—B3; 9 R—B4, R—Q3; 10 R—N5, QR—Q1; 11 R—Q5!, Resigns.** White wins the knight.

8

PETROSIAN'S ENDGAME

On his way to the world title in 1963, Tigran Petrosian became feared in international chess through his special skill in immobilizing his opponent's bishops. Certain openings, notably the Boleslavsky variation of the Sicilian (1 P—K4, P—QB4; 2 N—KB3, N—QB3; 3 P—Q4, P×P; 4 N×P, N—B3; 5 N—QB3, P—Q3; 6 B—K2, P—K4), and the white side of the King's Indian, were specially favoured as vehicles for Petrosian to create positions where the enemy bishop would be locked in behind a pawn chain, while Petrosian would have squares of the opposite colour to this pawn chain for his knights.

Thus, in the Boleslavsky variation, an early Petrosian game continued 7 N—N3, B—K2; 8 O—O, O—O; 9 B—K3, B—K3; 10 B—B3, P— QR4; 11 N—Q5, B×N; 12 P×B, N—N1; 13 P—QR4 (13 Q—Q3 is stronger), QN—Q2; 14 B—K2, N—N3; 15 P—QB4, N(N3)—Q2 (Pilnik v Petrosian, Buenos Aires 1954), and after the follow-up . . .P— QN3; and . . .N—B4, White's queen's flank was immobilized and his king's bishop had no scope, so that it was an easy matter for Black to progress on the other side of the board where he was virtually a pawn up.

In later years, Petrosian found that the Boleslavsky cannot be forced (White does better with the Richter Attack 6 B—KN5 or with Fischer's 6 B—QB4), but he has had better success with the immobilized bishop theme as White in the King's Indian Defence (1 P—Q4, N—KB3; 2 P—QB4, P—KN3; 3 N—QB3, B—N2). There, Petrosian's grand plan is to develop a bishop to KN5 and to tempt Black to advance . . .P— KR3; and preferably . . .P—KN4. This accomplished, White's pair of knights and his light-squared bishop have fine play on the weakened light squares, which can no longer be guarded by pawns.

Even if Petrosian does not win on the king's side, he can switch to the other flank and open up lines of attack there. The basic strength of his strategy is, however, that White is really playing for an endgame. Once the immobilized black bishop has been established, and once potential outposts are available for a white knight, any piece exchanges favour White (except for a swap of Black's lame bishop). The final stage of Petrosian's endgame occurs where the winning side has an active knight while his opponent has a locked-in or restricted bishop.

The concepts of Petrosian's endgame and of the fine winning chances with knight against 'bad' bishop are thoroughly known to most experienced masters. In practice, when a player falls into a Petrosian-type middle game or endgame, he holds on to as many other pieces as possible. This is why all of the Petrosian endgames in this chapter include rooks on the board.

The principles to be kept in mind in handling Petrosian's endgame can be summarized as follows:

1. Try to entice or drive the opposing pawns on one flank into a rigid, immobile formation, and on the same colour as the bishop on that flank. This usually means in practice that a player with White will try to lure Black's king's-side pawns on to dark squares and the queen's flank pawns on to light squares.

2. Entice the opponent to advance his pawns and so create holes in his position (a) by the development of a bishop at N5 in front of a fianchettoed enemy bishop, to encourage pawns to drive away the N5 bishop by P—R3 and P—N4; and (b) by the advance of a RP to R4 or R5, partly again to encourage the opponent's NP to come to N4 and partly because later on in a simplified ending there may be queening possibilities with the advanced RP.

3. Avoid giving the opponent any chance to swap his handicapped bishop.

4. Normally exchange off other pieces where possible, especially the opposing bishop which is not handicapped by the rigid pawn chain.

5. Infiltrate with the king along the squares of the opposite colour to the opposing bad bishop.

6. Maintain the initiative and restrict active counterplay to a minimum.

7. Look for outpost squares for knights on squares of the opposite colour to the enemy bad bishop.

A typical example of how Petrosian's endgame works against a co-operative opponent is this opening from Petrosian-Schweber, Stockholm Interzonal 1962.

1 P—Q4, N—KB3; 2 P—QB4, P—KN3; 3 N—QB3, B—N2; 4 P—K4, P—Q3; 5 B—K2, O—O; 6 B—N5 (principle 2(a) above) 6...P—KR3; 7 B—K3, P—K4; 8 P—Q5, P—B3; 9 P—KR4, P×P; 10 BP×P, QN—Q2; 11 P—R5 (principle 2(b) above) 11...P—KN4?; 12 P—B3, P—R3; 13 P—KN4, P—N4. See Diagram 158.

The chain of white pawns on the king's side holds Black's forces in complete subjugation. Black's queen's side is rather loose and potentially weak.

Petrosian usually looks world-weary when he's winning and from here to the end of the game his face never lost its expression of acute boredom.

14 P—R4

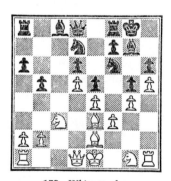

158. *White to play*

Petrosian begins to undermine and weaken Black's queen's-side pawns, again following principle 2(b).

14 . . .	P—N5
15 N—N1	P—R4
16 N—Q2	N—B4

17 B×N!

White gives up his 'good' bishop to create an additional queen's side weakness and, for the later stages of the ending, a potentially strong passed QP.

17 . . .	P×B
18 B—N5	B—N2
19 N—K2	N—K1
20 B×N!	

Now Black is left with two bad bishops against two good knights – the Petrosian endgame par excellence.

20 . . .	R×B
21 N—QB4	B—R3
22 Q—N3	Q—B3
23 R—QB1	B—KB1
24 N—N3	B—KB1

An admission of failure. After 24... B×N; 25 R×B, B—Q3, Black's apparently impregnable position would be stormed by White's plan of:

(a) placing his knight on KB5 and king on K2;
(b) doubling rooks on the QB file;
(c) playing Q—Q3 and P—N3;
(d) retreating the rook from QB4 to QB2.

After these steps Black would have no answer to the threats of Q—R6, Q—N5, N×B, and, if the bishop retreats from Q3, P—Q6.

25 O—O	R—Q1
26 K—N2	R—R2
27 R—KB2	K—R2
28 R(2)—B2	Q—R3?

28...B—R3 and B×N was the only way to prolong resistance.

29 N×KP	R—B2
30 N—B4	B—KN2
31 Q—Q3	K—N1
32 R—Q2	R—K2

See Diagram 159.

33 P—K5!

The simplest. Petrosian gives back the pawn in order to exchange down to a simple endgame win.

33 . . .	B×KP
34 N×B	R×N

159. *White to play*

35 Q×Q	B×Q
36 R×P	B—B1

Or 36...B—N2; 37 N—B5, K—R2; 38 R×P, R(1)×P; 39 R(5)×R, R×R; 40 R×R, B×R; 41 P—R5, and the QRP will cost Black his bishop.

37 R×P	P—B4
38 P×P	B×P
39 N×B	R×N
40 R—N5!	R(1)—KB1
41 P—Q6	R×R

41...R×P? costs a rook after 42 P—Q7.

42 P×R	K—B2
43 P—Q7	Resigns

43...R—Q1; 44 P—N6, K—K2; 45 P—N7, P—N6; 46 K—N3 is zugzwang.

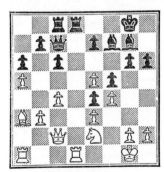

160. Petrosian *v* Savon
(U.S.S.R. Olympiad, 1972)
White to play

Only two pairs of minor pieces have been exchanged, but the position in

Diagram 160 is already effectively an endgame, since the major pieces are likely to be exchanged on the one open file. White has a decisive advantage because of his queen's-side bind which cannot be effectively challenged by Black. Even should Black succeed in exchanging the dark-squared bishops he will be left with a bad bishop against good knight ending.

1 B—B5!. Sealing the bind, and threatening to play 2 B—N6. **1... R×R ch; 2 Q×R, Q—Q1.** 2...R—Q1 can be met by 3 B—N6!, R×Q ch; 4 R×R, and 5 R—Q8 ch. **3 N—Q4, K—R2; 4 Q—K1, P—K3; 5 Q—N4.** Preventing the exchange of the dark-squared bishops, because the good knight versus bad bishop ending would be very difficult to win with rooks still on the board. **5...Q—Q2; 6 R—Q1, R—Q1; 7 B—N6, R—KN1; 8 Q—Q6, Q—K1.**

Black can do nothing to oppose the steady infiltration of White's pieces. If 8...Q×Q; 9 P×Q, and the passed QP is decisive. **9 N—B2, P—N4.** Passive defence would lose soon enough, so Black opens the KN file on to White's king, with little hope of making use of it. **10 Q—Q7, Q—KB1; 11 Q×NP, P×P; 12 R—Q8, B—K1; 13 P×P, K—R1.** The immobilization of Black's pieces is complete. **14 P—QN4!, P—R4.**

A last attempt to untangle his pieces. White now transposes to a won ending. **15 B—B5, Q—B2; 16 Q×Q, B×Q, and Black resigned.** He must lose more material after 17 R×R ch, K×R; 18 N—Q4.

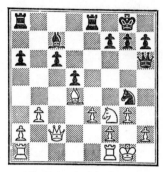

161. Petrosian v Belyavsky
(U.S.S.R. Championship, 1973)
White to play

Q, R×Q; **3 QR—B1, P—B3; 4 R—B2, N—K4; 5 B×N.** White's knight will prove much stronger than the bishop. **5...B×B; 6 R(1)—B1, R—QB1.** The QBP is adequately defended, so White now sets about improving his position.

7 R—B5, R—Q3. There was a threat of 8 R×QP. **8 R(1)—B2, K—B2; 9 K—B1, K—K3; 10 N—K1, P—Q5.** If Black waits passively, then White wins easily by transferring the knight to QN4. **11 P—B4, P—Q6; 12 R—Q2, B—N7; 13 R×P.** Not 13 R×B?, P—Q7. **13...R—QR1; 14 R×R ch, K×R; 15 N—Q3, P—QR4; 16 R—B4, B—R6.** White's advantage is overwhelming. He has an extra pawn, his pieces are far superior to Black's, and Black is still saddled with his pawn weaknesses. The rest is simple.

17 R—R4, B—B4; 18 N×B, K×N; 19 P—N4 ch, K—B5. If 19...K—N4; 20 R×P ch, gives White a simple winning king and pawn endgame. **20 R×P, R—QN1; 21 P—QR3, K—Q6; 22 K—B2, R—N2; 23 R—QB5, R—R2; 24 R×P, R×P; 25 K—B3, Resigns.**

White stands clearly better in Diagram 161 because of Black's weak pawns, especially the backward QBP. In order to exploit them, Petrosian finds a sharp tactical manoeuvre which first forces the exchange of queens, and then drives Black willy-nilly into Petrosian's endgame.

1 Q—KB5!, Q—K3. Black cannot avoid the exchange, since 1...Q—R6?; loses a pawn immediately to 2 Q×BP ch, K×Q; 3 N—N5 ch, and 4 N×Q. **2 Q×**

The example in Diagram 162 is instructive as revealing a difference in knowledge. Active international masters know the strength of Petrosian's ending and steer for it when given the chance in their own games, but a strong club player who knows about good knights

162. Kurajica v G. C. Taylor
(Evening Standard congress, London, 1973)
Black to play

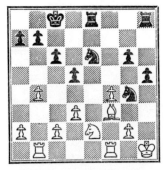

163. Gurgenidze v Petrosian
(Spartak team championship, 1961)
Black to play

and bad bishops, here underestimates the danger of defending this endgame, because he relies too much on the presence of rooks to guarantee a draw. **1...Q—R8 ch?.** Instead Black should try for a middle game attack with 1...P—QB4; or 1...QR—B1. **2 K—Q2, Q—R4; 3 Q×Q, P×Q.** White now stands better. Black has weak pawns on both flanks on the same coloured square as his bishop; while White, as is usual in Petrosian's endgame, also controls substantially more space. **4 K—B3, B—K1; 5 N—B4!.** White now attacks the QRP from the rank, not via the QR file as Black expected. White also drives black pawns on to light squares to entomb the black bishop, and maintain the underlying strategy of Petrosian's endgame. **5... P—R5; 6 R—K5, R—N4; 7 R(1)—K1, K—B1; 8 R×R, B×R; 9 R—K5, P—R3; 10 N—K3!, R—K1?.** 10...R—Q2 was relatively best. **11 N—Q5, R×R; 12 P×R, P—QB4.** If 12...P—QB3; 13 N—B4, P—N3; 14 K—Q4, P—R4; 15 K—B5 wins. Black is quite lost. **13 N—B4, P—N3; 14 N—Q3, P—B5; 15 N—B4, K—K2; 16 K—Q4, K—Q2; 17 P—QB3, K—K2; 18 K—Q5, K—Q2; 19 P—K6 ch, K—K2.** Or 19... P×P ch; 20 K—K5. **20 K—K5, B—B3; 21 N—Q5 ch, K—K1.** If 18...B×N; 19 K×B, gives White a winning king and pawn endgame. **22 K—Q6, B×N; 23 K×B, K—K2; 24 P×P, K×P; 25 K—Q6, P—R4; 26 P—B4, Resigns.**

Petrosian, the specialist in bad bishops, can sense when his opponent's bishop lacks mobility even when a superficial glance at the position suggests that the piece has reasonable scope. Gurgenidze permitted this position (Diagram 163) because he anticipated that Black's two chains of pawns on light squares would provide targets for his bishop; but in fact the bishop is handicapped by its own knight and pawns on light squares and can be quickly harried by the black knights. The icing on the cake is that, unusually in Petrosian's endgame, Black also has mating threats.

1...N—K6!; 2 KR—B1, P—KN4. The threat to win material brings Black's other knight into action with gain of tempo. **3 P×P, N(K3)×P; 4 N—Q4, P—R5; 5 N—B5.** White's king is close to being in a mating net. Petrosian pointed out 5 K—N1, P—R6; 6 P—N3, P—R7 ch; 7 K—R1, KR—B1; and White is defenceless. **5...N×B.** The simplest way to win. **6 N—Q6 ch.** Or 6 N×N, N—Q7. **6...K—N1; 7 N×R, N—Q7; 8 R—K1, N×BP; 9 N—Q6, N×R(N8); 10 R×N, R—KB1!.** Preventing the white knight from retreating. **11 P—N5, K—B2; 12 Resigns.**

Anatoly Karpov demonstrates, from Diagram 164, that his handling of the Petrosian endgame is in no way inferior

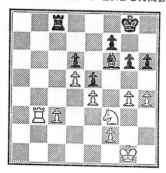

164. Karpov *v* Gligoric
(Interzonal, Leningrad, 1973)
White to play

to his skill in the Fischer endgame. Karpov has an extra pawn, but it is difficult to make progress as the extra pawn cannot yet be advanced. However, the key factor in the position is the superiority of the knight over Black's bishop, which outweighs Black's temporary advantage of active against passive rook.

1 K—N2!. Gradually improving his position – the knight is now protected, and the king brought closer to the centre. **1...P—R4.** 1...K—B1 would have been better. It is generally desirable to exchange pawns when behind in the ending, but here the result is only a weak KRP. **2 P×P, P×P; 3 R—N6!.** An extra pawn in the form of a protected passed QP is clearly stronger than a weak backward QBP. **3...R×P.** Black has no choice, because 3...B—Q2; loses to 4 R—B6, e.g. 4...R×R; 5 P×R, B—Q1; 6 N—N1!, K—B1; 7 N—K2, K—K1; 8 P—B7!, B×BP; 9 N—N3, or 4...R—R1; 5 P—B4, followed by P—B5.

4 R×P, K—N2; 5 R—B6, R—Q6. 5...R—R6, preserving the rook's flexibility, would be slightly better. **6 R—B7, K—N3; 7 R—B8, B—N2.** If 7...R—R6, then 8 R—K8, R—R5; 9 N×P ch, wins. **8 R—B6 ch!, K—R2.** Forced because other moves are met by 9 N×P ch. **9 N—N5 ch, K—N1; 10 R—B8 ch, B—B1; 11 R—B7.** Forcing another weakness. **11...P—B3; 12 N—K6.** Threatening to win the bishop, and trapping Black's king on the back rank.

12...B—R3; 13 R—Q7, R—Q7; 14 K—B1. 14 P—Q6 probably wins, but there is no rush and no need to give material away to 14...B—K6.

14...R—Q8 ch; 15 K—K2, R—Q7 ch; 16 K—K1, R—B7; 17 P—Q6!. Only now, having avoided material loss and deflected the black rook from the Q file. **17...R—B8 ch; 18 K—K2, R—B7 ch; 19 K—B1, R—B3; 20 K—N2, R—N3.** If 20...B—Q7, then 21 R—N7 ch, K—R1; 22 P—Q7, R—Q3; 23 R—K7, B—R4; 24 P—Q8=Q ch, B× Q; 25 R—K8 ch wins, while 20...R—B7 is met by 21 R—QB7!, R—Q7; 22 P—Q7.

21 N—B7!, R—N2. Or 21...B—B1; 22 N—K8. **22 N—Q5!, Resigns.** After 22...R×R; 23 N×P ch, K—B2; 24 N×R, K—K3; 25 N×P!, White is three pawns ahead.

165. Petrosian *v* Botvinnik
(5th match game, 1963)
White to play

Black cannot hold the QBP, and he also has king's-side pawn weaknesses. As in Diagram 163, the position in Diagram 165 is an instance where Black's bishop is not obviously a bad piece at first glance; some quite strong players might even aim for this position for Black, by over-estimating the value of the QBP with the bishop in support. But Petrosian notes that the bishop is squashed for space on the queen's side because of the pawns on QR2 and QN3. By forcing the black passed pawn to

QB6, where it restricts the bishop still further, White gains time for his king to invade the weakened pawns and squares on the other flank.

1 N—Q2, P—B6. After 1...B×N; 2 K×B, K—Q3; 3 K—B3, K—B4; 4 R—Q2! White wins. **2 N—K4, B—R4; 3 K—Q3, R—Q1 ch; 4 K—B4, R—Q8.** 4...R—Q7; is answered by 5 K—N3, but not 5 N×R?, P×N, and Black wins. **5 N×P, R—KR8; 6 N—K4!.** 6 P—KR3 was also possible, but Petrosian returns the pawn to improve the placing of his pieces. **6...R×P; 7 K—Q4, K—Q2.** Otherwise 8 R—B7 ch. **8 P—N3, B—N5; 9 K—K5, R—R4 ch; 10 K—B6, B—K2 ch; 11 K—N7.**

A fine example of an active king.

11...P—K4; 12 R—B6, R—R8; 13 K—B7, R—R8; 14 R—K6!, B—Q1. White wins quickly after 14...B—B4; 15 R×KP, R×P; 16 N×B ch, P×N; 17 R×P. **15 R—Q6 ch, K—B1; 16 K—K8, B—B2; 17 R—QB6, R—Q8.** Now if 17...R×P, then 18 N—B3, followed by 19 N—Q5, is decisive. **18 N—N5, R—Q1 ch; 19 K—B7, R—Q2 ch; 20 K—N8, Resigns.**

One of Petrosian's best endgame victories, and a wonderful combination of the Petrosian endgame with active use of the king.

166. Petrosian *v* Mecking
(*Wijk aan Zee*, 1971)
Black to play

Diagram 166 shows a middle game where both sides have weaknesses in their pawn structures, but Black's pieces are too cramped to take advantage of the light squares around White's king. White's pieces, in contrast, can be well posted on central squares to probe the holes in Black's position on both flanks. The middle game threats are used to switch into a Petrosian endgame, and incidentally to emphasize the point that Fischer's and Petrosian's endgames are more reliable winning techniques than a complex middle game where the opponent may suddenly create unexpected counter-chances.

1...P—R4. This move weakens more squares around Black's king, but it is the only way to prevent the dangerous 2 P—R5. White's plan is now clear: exchange the pieces, above all the dark-squared bishops, which can defend Black's weaknesses. **2 Q—B3, Q—Q1; 3 B—Q2, Q—K1?.** In the long run Black would not be able to prevent the exchange of bishops, but he should not acquiesce so easily in White's plans.

4 B—N5!, Q—Q1; 5 Q—B4, R—QB1; 6 R—K3, B×B; 7 P×B, R—R1; 8 Q—B6 ch, Q×Q; 9 KP×Q ch!. The right way to capture, maintaining a complete bind on the dark squares around Black's king, and freeing K5 for occupation by a piece. **9...K—R2; 10 K—N2, QR—K1; 11 P—KB4.** Preventing Black's liberating ...P—K4. **11... R—QN1; 12 R(3)—K1, N—N2.** Black can only effect the freeing move ...P—QN4 at the cost of the QRP. **13 R—R1, K—N1; 14 N—B3, N—Q3; 15 N—K5, B—K1.**

White has established complete control. The knight has been transferred to its strongest square, and in so doing has freed Q4 for his king. It only remains to open up the lines on the queen's side and Black is defenceless. **16 B—Q3, R—B1; 17 K—B3, B—B3; 18 R—KR2, B—K1; 19 K—K3, R—B2; 20 K—Q4.** See Diagram 167.

White's control, especially of the dark squares, has been increased to the maximum.

20...N—N2; 21 P—QN4. The break comes only now that White has established total control. **21...N—Q1; 22 R—R4, N—N2; 23 R—QR2, N—Q3; 24 R—KR1, N—N2; 25 P—N5, N—B4;**

167. *Black to play*

26 B—B2, N—Q2; 27 R—QR3, N—B4;
28 P—B4, N—Q2; 29 R—QB3, N×N;
30 K×N, P×P; 31 B—K4, R—B1; 32
R(1)—QB1, Resigns.
Black is helpless against White's
infiltration to the eighth rank, e.g.
32...P—R5; 33 P×P, R×P; 34 R×P,
R×R; 35 R×R, R—R1 (the only way
to defend the bishop); 36 R—B8, K—
R2; 37 B—B6, B×B; 38 R×R ch,
K×R; 39 P×B, and the pawn queens.

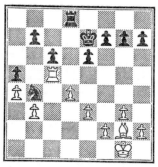

168. Doda *v* Geller
(European team championship,
Bath, 1973)
Black to play

It is not obvious at first sight in
Diagram 168, that White has a bad
bishop against Black's knight, since
White's central and king's-side pawn
chain is ideally arranged on the opposite
colour to his bishop. But the real action
is taking place on the other flank, where
White's QRP and QNP are weak, and
his bishop has no scope.
The ensuing play shows a special form

of the Petrosian endgame where a rook
and knight combine to invade the
enemy position and the defending
bishop has insufficient squares to dodge
their attack. Another key factor is the
superior centralization of Black's king.
    1...P—QN3; 2 R—B1. 2 R—B4 is
more accurate, to allow the king to come
across in defence of the QNP. 2...P—
QB4!; 3 P×P, N—Q6; 4 R—N1, N×
QBP; 5 P—QN4, N×P; 6 P×P, P×P;
7 R—R1, N—B6; 8 R×P, R—Q8 ch;
9 B—B1, N—K5; 10 K—N2. Otherwise
10...N—Q7. **10...R—Q7; 11 R—
R7 ch, K—B3; 12 R—R4, K—K4.** If
12...N×BP, then 13 R—KB4 ch.
    **13 K—N1, N×BP; 14 R—KB4, N—
Q8; 15 R×P, N×P; 16 B—R3.** 16 R×
P, K—B3; 17 R×P, R—Q8 wins the
bishop. **16...P—N4!; 17 P—N4.** Otherwise 17...P—N5. **17...P—R3; 18 R—
KR7, N—B7!.** Black is a pawn up, but
the decisive factor is his good knight
against the poor bishop. **19 B—N2, N—
K8; 20 B—N7, R—QN7; 21 B—R8,
R—R7; 22 B—B6, R—R3; 23 B—N5,
R—R7; 24 B—B6.** If 24 R×P, N—
B6 ch wins, e.g. 25 K—R1, K—B5; 26
B—B1, P—K4!.
    **24...R—QB7; 25 B—N7, R—QN7;
26 B—R8, R—QN1; 27 B—N7, K—B5;
28 K—B1, N—Q6; 29 P—R3, K—N6;
30 B—K4, N—B7; 31 B—B6.** 31 B—
N2?, R—N8 ch. **31...R—N3; 32 Resigns.**

So far we have only looked at
Petrosian's endgame in its pure form
of rook and good knight against rook
and bad bishop. But as Diagram 169
shows, the combination of active rook
and bishop against passive rook and
bishop for the opponent can also be a
decisive advantage, even when there are
bishops of opposite colours.
    White is here a pawn up, but it is not
easy to create a passed pawn, and he
must beware of Black's drawing chances
if the rooks are exchanged. Nevertheless,
Petrosian shows that this endgame is an
easy win for White. Black's bad bishop
is combined with pawn weaknesses,

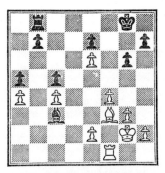

169. Petrosian *v* Matulovic
(*Sarajevo*, 1972)
White to play

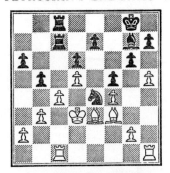

169A. Karpov *v* Kavalek
(Olympiad, *Nice*, 1974)
White to play

especially the QNP, and White can also seize the open Q file.

1 R—Q1, K—B1; 2 R—Q7, P—N3; 3 B—Q5, K—K1; 4 P—K4, P—R3; 5 K—B3. White has improved the position of all his pieces, while Black has only been able to centralize his king. **5. . .K—B1; 6 P—K5, P—KN4.** This helps White a little. 6. . .B—Q5; was slightly better, avoiding further pawn weaknesses.

7 K—K4, P×P; 8 P×P, K—K1; 9 P—B5, R—B1. Black is very short of moves, e.g. 9. . .B—Q5; 10 B—B6!, K—B1; 11 P—B6, and wins easily, as 11. . .P×P; 12 P×P, B×P is not possible on account of 13 R—B7 ch. **10 R—N7, R—Q1.** Black has nothing constructive to do, e.g. 10. . .B—Q5; 11 B—B6 ch, K—B1; 12 B—Q7, R—Q1; 13 B—B6, R—B1; 14 P—B6, P×P; 15 P×P, B×P; 16 R—B7 ch, K—N1; 17 B—Q7, winning the bishop. **11 P—B6, P×P; 12 B—B6 ch, K—B1; 13 P—K7 ch, Resigns.**

The technique of winning an opposite coloured bishops ending with rook and active bishop against rook and passive bishop has been further developed since the relatively simple example of Petrosian *v* Matulovic (where Black's position was already bad at the start of the ending). Anatoly Karpov, playing the prestige top board game against Lubomir Kavalek of the United States in the Nice

Olympiad, 1974, refined Petrosian's idea into a more sophisticated winning technique. The strategy and play from Diagram 169A well deserves the title of Karpov's ending.

At first sight in Diagram 169A Black has good counterplay on the QB file to balance White's active king and his space advantage on the king's side. In fact, the position is won for White, and Karpov's precision play to prove it is very instructive.

1 P—KN4!. Forcing Black towards the Karpov endgame. Instead, both 1 BP×P?, R—B6 ch, and 1 B×N?, P× B ch; 2 K×P, P×BP give Black good counterplay. **1. . .P×P ch; 2 R×P, R× R; 3 P×R.** The swap of a pair of rooks has deprived Black of any chance of invading the white position via the QN file.

3. . .N—B4 ch. After 3. . .R—N1 White would go for the Karpov endgame by 4 B×N, P×B ch; 5 K×P, R—N7; 6 P—R6, B—B1; 7 P—N5, when Black is, for practical purposes, a bishop down. **4 B×N!.** A key move. Many masters in such an ending would automatically preserve White's bishop pair. **4. .R×B; 5 P—R6, B—B1.** The bishop has to abandon the long diagonal, since 5. . . B—R1 would be neatly met by 6 R— QN1, K—B2; 7 R—N8, B—R8; 8 P×P, P×P; 9 B—R5 ch, K—B3; 10 R—B8 mate. **6 K—B3!.** This is more precise than 6 P—N5, when Black could get counterplay by R—R4 and R—R6 ch. With his king move, Karpov is ready to answer R—R4 by K—N3, and again he threatens P—N5 followed by a rook invasion down the QN file.

6...P×P; 7 B×P, K—B2; 8 B—K6 ch, K—B3; 9 B—N8, R—B2; 10 B×P. The Karpov endgame establishes a decisive passed pawn. 10...P—K3;11 B—N8, P×P; 12 P—R7, B—N2. A better try is 12...R×P ch; 13 K—Q3, B—N2; 14 P—R8=Q, B×Q; 15 R×B, K—N2 (or 15...R×P; 16 B×P); 16 B×P, R—B4; 17 R—N8 ch, K—B3; 18 B—N3, but White should still win. 13 B×P, B—R1; 14 K—Q3, K—B4; 15 K—K3, R—

K2 ch; 16 K—B3, P—R4; 17 P—R4, R—QB2; 18 B—K4 ch, K—B3; 19 R—R6, R—KN2; 20 K—N4, Resigns.

If 20...K—B2; 21 K—N5, K—K2; 22 R—R1, K—B2; 23 B—Q5 ch, K—B1; 24 R—QN1, R×P; 25 R—N8 ch, K—N2; 26 R—N8 mate. Just as in Diagram 169, the final stage of winning this type of endgame is for the stronger side's king, rook and bishop to invade the enemy position and combine in a mating attack which the 'passive bishop' player, who is for practical purposes a piece down, cannot defend.

Active versus Passive Knight

In recent years, the Petrosian endgame proper with rook and knight against rook and locked-in bishop has scored fewer successes for its inventor. Too many opponents are too well primed. But there is another variant, less well known. The theme is rook and active knight against rook and passive knight, and its strength is shown in diagrams 170-172.

170. Gligoric *v* Andersson
(Olympiad, Skopje, 1972)
White to play

1 P—R4. White has a clear advantage because of his much superior knight and more aggressive rook. 1...R—R5. To tie the white knight down. 2 P—N3, P—R3; 3 K—N2, R—B5; 4 K—B1, R—B1; 5 N—Q2, R—Q1; 6 N—N3, R—Q2; 7 R—N8, K—B2; 8 N—B5, R—R2; 9 N—N7. Threatening 10 N—Q8 ch, followed by 11 N—B6 ch or 11 N×P according to Black's reply.

9...K—N1; 10 N—Q6!, R—R5?.

Keeping the rook on the second rank would have made White's task more difficult. 11 R—N7, R×P; 12 N—K8, R—K5; 13 R×P ch, K—R1; 14 P—B4, R—R5; 15 N—K7!. Stronger than 15 R—KB7, K—N1; 16 R—K7, N—R2, when Black has some chances of hanging on. Black resigns.

White follows up with N—B6, Black's rook is forced to return to the back rank by the threat of R—KB7, and then White's king penetrates with decisive effect to K7.

White stands clearly better in Diagram 171 and can immediately make further progress, strengthening his grip on the QB file and driving the black knight out of play.

1 P—QN4!. The knight is not allowed to stay on its good central square. 1...N—R3; 2 P—QR3, R—B2; 3 P—R3. A precautionary move – having obtained the advantage in this type of position, there is rarely any need to rush things. 3...R×R; 4 Q×R, N—B2. To re-centralise his knight on Q4.

171. Polugaevsky *v* Rashkovsky
(41st U.S.S.R. championship, 1973)
White to play

5 N—Q4, N—Q4; 6 Q—B4, Q—N2;
7 R—B1, P—QR3. Black is tied passively
to defence. This weakens his queen's-
side pawns, but otherwise P—N5
followed by Q—B6 is very strong. **8
Q—B6, Q×Q; 9 R×Q, K—B1; 10 P—
QR4, R—N1; 11 P—N5, P×P; 12
P×P, R—N2; 13 R—B8 ch, K—K2; 14
P—K4, N—B2; 15 P—K5, P—B3.** No
better is 15...N—Q4, which allows 16
N—B6 ch, K—Q2; 17 R—B8 winning.
16 N—B6 ch, Resigns.
  16...K—Q2; 17 R—Q8 is mate,
and 16...K—B2 loses the rook to 17
N—Q8 ch.

In the decisive game of his candidates'
match against Lajos Portisch, Petrosian
won by a concealed and more sophisticated version of Polugaevsky's technique against Rashkovsky. Portisch
must have thought that his move ...Q—
KB5 which brought about Diagram 172
gained the initiative, but Petrosian
judged that his better king position,

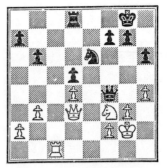

172. Petrosian *v* Portisch
(13th game, Candidates' quarter-final,
1974)
White to play

control of the open QB file, and Portisch's
ineffective knight, between them added
to full value for a pawn minus.
  **1 P×Q!, N×P ch; 2 K—N3, N×Q;
3 R—B3!.** Black's knight can be made
more passive before the white rook
invades the seventh. **3...N—N5?.** After
3...N—N7, Petrosian would have re-
peated moves for a draw by 4 R—B2,
N—Q6; 5 R—B3, N—N7, but Black
still did not realize his danger.
  4 P—R3, N—R3; 5 P—N4, N—N1.
A better chance is 5...R—Q2; 6 P—N5,
N—B2; 7 N—K5, R—K2; 8 N—B6,
R—K8. **6 R—B7, P—QR4; 7 P—N5.**
White's pieces are all active while
Black's are passive, especially his knight.
7...N—Q2; 8 K—B4, P—R4; 9 N—
K5!, N—B1. 9...N×N; 10 K×N
would be hopeless. **10 R—N7.** Not 10
R×P?, N—N3 ch!.
  10...P—B3; 11 N—B6. Black can no
longer put up any meaningful resistance.
**11...N—N3 ch; 12 K—N3, R—Q3; 13
R×QNP, R—K3; 14 R—N8 ch, N—
B1; 15 R—R8, R—K8; 16 N—Q8, K—
R2; 17 P—N6, R—QN8; 18 P—N7, N—
Q2; 19 R×P, Resigns.**

To conclude this and the previous chapter, here is the answer to the
question which some readers will by now be asking. What happens
when the Fischer endgame and the Petrosian endgame come face to
face?

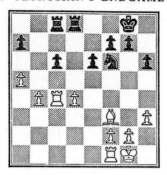

173. Fischer *v* Petrosian
(Interzonal, Stockholm, 1962)
Black to play

In Diagram 173, both sides have weaknesses, but Black manages to hang on.

1...N—Q4; 2 R(1)—B1, R—N1. Passive defence by 2...R—Q3, fails immediately to 3 P—N5. **3 R×P, R×P; 4 R—B8, R×R; 5 R×R ch, K—R2; 6 R—QR8, R—N2; 7 P—R6, R—Q2; 8 R—QN8.** Threatening to force a win by 9 R—N7.

8...R—Q3; 9 B—K2, N—B2. The knight's agility enables Black to simplify. **10 R—N7, N×P; 11 R×BP, N—N5; 12 R×RP, R×P; 13 B—N4, R—Q3; 14 R—K7, N—Q4; 15 R×KP, R×R; 16 B×R, N—B3; draw agreed.** The ending is a theoretical draw.

9

ADJUDICATION TECHNIQUES

Many games in match competition are decided by adjudication. As 30 or 36 moves in a session are common, it is almost certain that any endgame that develops will not be resolved by the players, but be left to the adjudicator. When this happens several types of situation are possible.

The key fact to remember is that an adjudicator, confronted with a position in which one side is a pawn up for which the opponent has no compensation, will normally give the win to the player with the extra material. To be a pawn up in a position for adjudication (your opponent having no compensation), is as good as being, say, a rook up in a game played to a finish. The point should be quite an automatic one if the adjudicator knows his job. If he does not know his job, then it is up to the strongest player in your club to make an official appeal.

In a game therefore in which adjudication may be involved you should consider, when coming up to about move 20 or 24, that any material plus (without positional compensation for the opponent) is a near-decisive advantage; far more so than when a game is played to a finish.

What about, though, the more difficult situation where you have a positional advantage but there is no material advantage? Playing recently in league chess for the first time for some years, I developed a conscious approach to such situations. It seemed to me that the correct technique is a kind of 'window-dressing' of your position. During the last few moves before adjudication, you should put your pieces on the most active squares possible. Adjudicators will be impressed, other things being equal, by just the general look of a position. If one side's pieces are on active squares and the other side's passive, you may get a win even though material is equal. As an example, take the following game where Black, being the lower-graded player, quite correctly made as few moves as possible, in fact, the minimum thirty moves:

Barden v A. Heaton (Middlesex League, 1973). 1 P—K4, P—K4; 2 N—KB3, N—QB3; 3 B—N5, P—QR3; 4 B—R4, N—B3; 5 O—O, P—QN4; 6 B—N3, B—K2; 7 R—K1, P—Q3; 8 P—QR4, R—QN1; 9 P×P, P×P; 10 P—B3, B—N5; 11 P—R3, B—R4; 12 P—Q3, Q—Q2; 13 QN—Q2, P—N4; 14 N—B1, R—N1; 15 N—N3, P— KN5; 16 N×B, N×N; 17 N—R2, N—B3; 18 N×P, N×N; 19 P×N, Q×P; 20 Q×Q, R×Q; 21 B—K3, N—Q1; 22 P—N3, K—Q2; 23 B—Q1, R—N1; 24 K—N2, N—K3; 25 R—R1, R—KN2 (see Diagram 174). 26 K—B3, B—N4; 27 B×B, N×B ch; 28 K—K3, N—K3; 29 P—QN4, K—Q1; 30 B—N3, K—Q2; 31 R—KR6.

174. *White to play*

175. *The final position*

Diagram 175 shows the final position before adjudication. White's last few moves were all part of the technique of 'window-dressing'. He brought the king up to K3, advanced the QNP and moved the bishop behind it to QN3, and finally, on move 31, the last move of the game, put the rook on the impressive-looking square KR6, where it ties down Black's weak KRP and also gets some indirect pressure on the knight at K3. Later analysis showed that White had good winning chances by playing P—Q4 and possibly P—Q5, and then moving the bishop round to Q3 with threats to the artificially isolated black QNP, but in any case this was not necessary since the adjudicator gave the position a win for White.

'Window-dressing' is even more important in weekend tournaments – the judge can very rarely spend much time on these positions.

Another facet of adjudication situations is that you may be in a middle game at the end of the session, but analysis will show variations where you can go into an ending. In that case the middle game and the endgame have to be treated as a whole. As an illustration, diagram 176 shows a position from the 1973 *Sunday Times* National Schools Tournament between R. C. Picot (Whitgift) and P. F. Stoney (Maidenhead Grammar) on which the result of a match depended.

The position in Diagram 176 is a middle game situation with apparently a lot of play and apparently also nothing demonstrable. White's only advantage is, seemingly, that the black queen is rather out of the game. However, analysis showed that White could combine the attack on the queen's file with various threats to the black queen, and also, in some variations, with a king's-side attack. For our purpose the most important aspect is that some variations transposed rather swiftly into an ending.

The analysis took some 20 hours' work; this was a difficult position. It showed that after 1 KR—Q1, P—R4; 2 R—Q4, Black's best chance to save his queen and also avoid decisive trouble on the queen's file was to play 2...Q—N7, and then 3 R(1)—B4, Q—N8; 4 Q—KB3. Now in this position Black's only chance is to go into an endgame by 4...K—N2, with the idea of exchanging queens on his KB4 and, if the white rook then attacks the KRP, to defend it by 5...K—N3. That is the immediate tactical point of 4...K—N2.

The original position was adjudicated a draw, which is normal procedure in a position where no winning line is clear. Nevertheless, it is possible to demonstrate that Black is forced to go into this endgame by bringing his queen back to

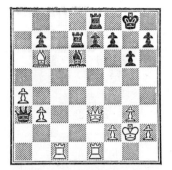

176. *White to play*

KB4. The appeal judge in fact saw this possibility of bringing the queen back and on the strength of that turned down the appeal without going on to analyse the ending.

Yet the appeal was correct. White's pin on the queen's file is strong enough to give a decisive advantage in the ending because now a concealed factor in the position comes into play; White has a 2–1 pawn majority on the queen's side and this, supported by the strong bishop on QN6, will enable him to advance his QRP to QR7 and obtain a winning position.

Thus from diagram 176:

1 KR—Q1 P—R4

The appeal judge did not look too carefully. He suggested 1...Q—R7?, but this is refuted by 2 Q—Q3, threatening both 3 Q—N5, and, more drastically, 3 R—B2, Q—R6; 4 B—B5. The tactical trick 2...B—B4 fails to 3 Q×R, Q× BP ch; 4 K—R3, when the white queen stops 4...Q—KB4 and threatens 5 Q× R ch.

2 R—Q4	Q—N7
3 R(1)—B4	Q—N8
4 Q—KB3	K—N2

At this point the appeal judge noted that 'White has an obvious advantage, but no clear win can be demonstrated.' The natural next step for any adjudicator is to see whether there are any forcing variations to take advantage of Black's weaknesses – the offside queen, the king position weakened by ...P—KR4, the

pinned bishop, and the stalemated rook on Q2.

Black's intention is to play 5...Q—B4, with the idea that, after the exchange of queens, he can answer R—KR4 by ...K—N3.

5 R—Q1

Forcing Black to carry out his 'threat'.

5 ...	Q—B4
6 Q×Q	P×Q

177. *White to play*

White can now make use of his queen's-side majority in the ending.

7 P—QN4

This advance of the queen's-side majority is the natural plan. Black has to spend several moves before he can unravel the traffic jam on the queen's file.

7 ...	K—B3

The other try, 7...P—K4, fails to 8 R—B2 (8 P—N5, is also possible), and now if 8...K—B3; 9 R(2)—Q2, K—K3; 10 P—N5, R(1)—K2; 11 P—R5, B—N1; 12 R×R, R×R; 13 R×R, K×R; 14 P—R6 wins.

8 P—N5	R—QR1

Or 8...K—K3; 9 P—R5, B—K4; 10 R×R, K×R; 11 P—R6, P×P; 12 P×P, R—QB1; 13 P—R7, R—QR1; 14 K—B3, and White has a normal technical win by advancing his king to QN7.

9 P—R5	K—N3
10 K—B3	K—B3
11 R—Q3	K—N3

178. *White to play*

Now Black is unable to prevent White from fulfilling his plan by the king march K—K2—Q1—B2—N3 (to allow the rooks to penetrate to the eighth rank

by preventing threats to the QRP from ...B—N5 at any stage), followed by the manoeuvre R—Q2, R(2)—B2, and R—B8, when the QRP is once again free to march – see diagram 179.

179.

So, from the position in diagram 176, we see that in adjudication and in appeals against adjudication you have to be prepared to switch your ideas from a middle game into an ending just as in the 'endgame openings' discussed in the following chapter. In the middle game the strong player, at all times, and the club player when it comes to a difficult adjudication, has to think of chances to switch into a winning ending.

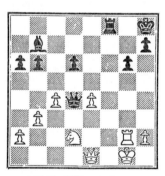

180. *White to play*

Diagram 180 shows a position for adjudication from an inter-club match played in 1973. Black was awarded the win, mainly because of his active pieces and the chances of preparing an advance of the king's-side pawns to open up mating possibilities against the white king. Black's last move before adjudication was the 'window-dressing' Q—Q5 ch, which established his queen on a strong central square. A typical middle game style of continuation from this

position is: **1 K—R1, R—B5; 2 R—K2, K—N2; 3 P—KR3, P—KN4; 4 Q—N3, P—R3. 5 K—R2, Q—K4; 6 R—N2, K—N3; 7 K—N1, Q—B3; 8 P—KR4, P—N5; 9 N—B3, K—R4,** when White is running out of moves.

What about the endgame into which White can transpose by **5 Q—K3** (instead of 5 K—R2), **Q×Q; 6 R×Q, K—B3?**. White appealed against the verdict, partly on the grounds that Black cannot force a king entry because of **7 K—N2.** If Black replies with 7...K—K4? this is answered adequately by 8 N—B3 ch. However, this is now a Fischer endgame (see Chapter 7) in which Black can make progress by utilizing his 2-1 pawn majority on the king's side, and creating an outside passed pawn whose advance can be supported by the king, bishop, and rook. The pawn then acts as a decoy which ties down White's pieces to passive defence, and enables the black king to penetrate on the other flank.

A typical line after 7 K—N2 is **7...P—KR4; 8 K—N3, P—R5 ch; 9 K—N2, P—N5; 10 P×P, R×P ch** (10...K—N4 is also possible); **11 K—R3** (if **11 K—B3**, **B—B1**, and the black king gets at the queen's-side pawns via the dark squares), **B—B1** and White is gradually forced back.

The above example serves to show that the window-dressing technique recommended in this chapter is not just a piece of advertising designed to impress a credulous adjudicator. A window-dressing move which improves the position of the pieces is likely to mean that the adjudicator, or the appeal judge, who examines endings which result from the middle game position at adjudication time, is more likely to find winning lines from the more active situation of the window-dresser's forces.

181. *White to play*

Diagram 181 was reached at adjudication time in the semi-finals of the 1969 *Sunday Times* National Schools Tournament, between C. C. W. Shephard (King Edward's, Birmingham) and M. P. Townsend (Trinity, Croydon), and decided a place in the finals. White (to move) judged that his queen's-side majority was more valuable than Black's KNP in a pawn endgame, but left the actual analysis to the adjudicators. It was a sound decision, because in over-the-board play it would be possible to mishandle the exact timing required to demonstrate the win. The adjudicator, however, agreed with White and gave him the win.

White wins by: **1 N—K4 ch, N×N; 2 K×N, K×P; 3 P—N4, P×P; 4 P×P, K—R5.** Best. If the king goes to R6, White's QBP will queen with check, while if it goes to KR4, then both sides queen but White captures the black queen by checks on the KR and KN files. **5 P—B5, P—KN4; 6 P—N5, P—N5; 7 P—B6, P×P; 8 P×P, P—N6; 9 K—B3, P—K5 ch; 10 K—N2!, P—K6; 11 K—B3!,** and White wins.

We can summarize this chapter with a recipe for playing in league chess with adjudications. If you are the weaker player, your endgame technique should be to steer for endings in which you have a positional rather than a material disadvantage, in the hope that by adjudication time this will not be decisive. If you are the stronger player you ideally need to be a pawn up with no compensation. Failing that, if your advantage is only positional, you should, in the first instance, make your position look as aggressive and impressive as possible by move 30 or 36, and also be prepared to devote several hours of concrete analysis to demonstrate a winning situation, either at the time of sending in the adjudication or on appeal, if you are not given a win in the first instance.

Too many average players simply assume that the adjudicator is infallible, or, that it is somehow not ethical to contest his decision. This is not so. An ambitious player who wishes to improve at chess, and has only league chess to do so, must take all opportunities to increase his number of points. There is no essential difference between trying to win by adjudication in league chess and analysing a postal game which, say on move 20, many correspondence players will analyse down to move 30 or 35, looking for winning endings all the time. Therefore adjudication technique is a much under-estimated aspect of endgame play, and it is hoped that the ideas in this chapter will enable readers to increase their percentage of wins in league chess.

A really ambitious team may even adopt slightly dubious techniques to ensure wins on adjudication. When I was match captain of Oxfordshire in the 1951 County Championship final against Middlesex, it was clear about ten minutes before adjudication time that the match might well depend on a difficult endgame in progress on a lower board where the Oxfordshire player, a rather nervous Swedish student I. Galvenius, was opposed by the experienced former international player J. Stone. The Oxfordshire top boards had finished their games and our number one player, Canadian champion D. A. Yanofsky, pointed out to me that our Swedish player had his hand hovering over a piece and that this could well be a decisive error . . . What I did as match captain was to announce in a loud voice, just by Galvenius's ear, 'It is five minutes to go to adjudication time.' Galvenius's hand jumped in the air and he did not make any move between then and adjudication time. The position went for adjudication, and after three days of analysis by the Oxfordshire top boards (Yanofsky, Tylor, Barden, and Persitz) a clever winning line was found, depending on a single tempo in an ending of rook against three pawns. The position was given a win for the Oxfordshire player, and on that game the County Championship was decided.

10

ENDGAME OPENINGS

The theory behind a number of opening systems is partly based on the possibilities of transposing rapidly into a favourable endgame. When using such opening systems the strong player is constantly considering the features of the position in front of him in terms of the endgame; concentrating on the centralization of his king and the avoidance of weakening pawn moves. The most notable of these systems is the Exchange Variation of the Ruy Lopez.

Ruy Lopez—Exchange Variation

We will start by considering one of the basic positions, arising after: **1 P—K4, P—K4; 2 N—KB3, N—QB3; 3 B—N5, P—QR3; 4 B ×N, QP ×B; 5 P—Q4.** 5 O—O, an example of which is on p. 118, is the most popular continuation nowadays, but 5 P—Q4, also leads to similar positions. **5. . .P ×P; 6 Q ×P, Q ×Q; 7 N ×Q.** See Diagram 182.

182. *Black to play*

White has released the tension very early and has conceded Black the two bishops. White's long-term idea is that if all the pieces are removed from the board he has a very great advantage in the ending thanks to his *mobile* king's-side pawn majority. White can ulti-

mately create a healthy passed pawn, while Black's queen's-side majority cannot, on its own, force a passed pawn.

The first Lasker *v* Tarrasch 1908 World Championship match game continued (from Diagram 182):

7 . . .	P—QB4
8 N—K2	B—Q2
9 P—QN3	B—B3
10 P—KB3	B—K2
11 B—N2	B—B3

11. . .N—B3, retaining the two bishops is better, rather than obliging White by helping him to exchange towards a favourable ending.

12 B × B	N × B
13 N—Q2	O—O—O
14 O—O—O	R—Q2
15 N—KB4	R—K1
16 N—B4	

115

White threatens to force another favourable exchange with N—QR5.

16 . . .	P—QN3
17 P—QR4	P—QR4
18 R×R	N×R
19 R—Q1	N—K4

Allowing White to exchange another pair of pieces, bringing him still closer to the desired king and pawn ending.

| 20 N×N | R×N |
| 21 P—B4 | |

It is precisely this pawn formation (and also the pawns on QR2, QN3, and QB2) that prevents Black from ever forcing a passed pawn on the queen's side by use of his pawns alone. White ignores any black pawn advance, never capturing, only recapturing.

| 21 . . . | R—K1 |

21...R—K2 is rather better, so that if 22 N—R5, then P—B3.

| 22 N—R5 | R—N1 |
| 23 R—Q3 | P—B3 |

White now sets about centralizing his king – it is needed to help shepherd through the king's-side majority.

24 K—Q2	B—K1
25 N—N3	B—Q2
26 K—K3	R—K1

Now that the king is centralized, Lasker starts his general king's-side advance.

| 27 N—R5 | R—K2 |
| 28 P—KN4 | P—B3 |

Black prepares, in vain, for a queen's-side advance. It would have been better to hurry over to the king's side with the king.

| 29 P—R4 | K—B2 |
| 30 P—N5? | |

30 K—B4! was the most accurate.

| 30 . . . | P—B4 |

30...P×P; 31 P×P is distinctly worse, as it would allow White to force a pair of connected passed pawns.

31 N—N3	P×P
32 N×P	B—B4
33 P—R5	R—Q2
34 R—B3	

34 R×R ch, K×R draws – the blocked pawn position would not allow White's king any entry squares.

| 34 . . . | R—Q8 |
| 35 K—B4 | |

183. *Black to play*

| 35 . . . | B—Q2? |

Black misses the draw which was possible here, following White's inaccurate move 30, by 35...B×N!; 36 P×B, K—Q3!, and White's king has no entry squares; or 36 K×B, R—KR8; 37 R—Q3, R×P; 38 K—B5, P—R3; 39 P—B4, P×P; 40 K—N6, R—R5; 41 P×P, P—N4!; 42 BP×P (White has nothing better than this anti-positional move, e.g. 42 K×P, P×BP; 43 P×P, R×P), 42...P×P; 43 P×P, K—N3; 44 K×P, K×P; 45 P—N6, P—R5; 46 P×P ch, R×P; 47 R—KN3, P—B5; 48 K—B6, K—N5; 49 P—N7, R—R1, and draws.

36 R—K3!	R—KR8
37 N—N3	R—R5 ch
38 K—K5	R—R6
39 P—B4	K—Q1

If 39...B—N5, then 40 P—B5, B× RP; 41 K—K6, and White's king can shepherd home the KBP, e.g. 41...R—R7; 42 N×B, R×N; 43 P—B6, and wins.

40 P—B5	R—R5
41 P—B6	P×P ch
42 K×P	B—K1
43 N—B5!	

184. *Black to play*

43 . . .   R—R8

43...R×RP loses instantly to 44 R×B ch!, K×R; 45 N—N7 ch. But now the pawns cannot be stopped.

44	P—N6	P×P
45	P×P	R—KN8
46	R×B ch	K×R
47	P—N7	K—Q2
48	N—R4	R×P

Otherwise the knight goes to KN6.

49	K×R	K—K3
50	N—B3	K—B4
51	K—B7	K—K5
52	K—K6!	K—Q6

No time to capture the knight.

53	K—Q6	K—B6
54	K×P	K×P
55	K—N5	Resigns

Shortly before this game took place Emanuel Lasker set up the position after White's seventh move, and asked his namesake Edward Lasker 'Can you tell me how anyone can lose that opening?' He was, of course, referring to 'anyone' with the white pieces.

In the above game Tarrasch overlooked one drawing resource, but Black faces very difficult problems, as is shown by the following sample analysis by ex-World Champion Dr Euwe.

The position in Diagram 185 has the same pawn structure as Diagram 182, the only difference being that all the pieces have been removed.

White has excellent winning chances

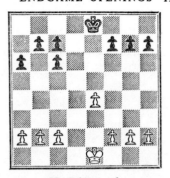

185. *White to play*

in this ending: 1 K—K2, K—K2; 2 K—K3, K—K3; 3 P—KB4, P—QB4; 4 P—B4!, P—QB3; 5 P—QR4, P—QN4; 6 P—QN3!. If 6 RP×P?, then 6...BP×P; 7 P×P, P×P, and Black, after freeing his doubled pawns, also threatens to obtain a passed pawn at his first opportunity. 6...P—B3; 7 P—R5, P—N5; 8 P—N4, P—N4. Averbakh and Maizelis suggest 8...P—N3, trying to blockade the centre. 9 P—K5!, NP×P ch. 9...BP×P is answered by 10 P×NP.

10 K×P, P×P ch; 11 K—K4, P—R3; 12 P—R4, K—B3; 13 P—N5 ch, P×P; 14 P×P ch, K×P. 14...K—K3 is met with 15 K×P, K—N6. 15 K×P, K—N5; 16 K—Q6, K—B5; 17 K×P, K—K5; 18 K×P, K—Q6; 19 K×P, K—Q5; 20 K—R3. 20 K—R4, also works, but not 20 P—B5?, K—Q4!. 20...K—B4; 21 K—R4, K—Q5. Otherwise 22 P—N4. 22 K—N4, K—K4; 23 K—B5, and wins.

The modern treatment of this opening contains some refinements. White keeps the option of playing a middle game in which his attack on Black's queen's-side castled king generally proves stronger than Black's threats on the other flank. If the queens stay on the board, White can also treat the middle game by relying on his space superiority and the activity of his minor pieces on the dark squares, especially QB5 in front of Black's doubled pawns. But the Exchange Variation of the 1970s still relies principally on the idea of swapping down into a superior endgame.

1 P—K4, P—K4; 2 N—KB3, N—QB3; 3 B—N5, P—QR3; 4 B×N, QP× B; 5 O—O is the modern treatment. For the main illustration of White's strategy, we follow Fischer *v* Unzicker, Siegen Olympiad 1970, see Diagram 186.

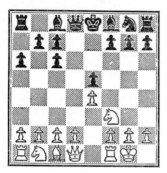

186. *Black to play*

5 . . .   P—B3

5...Q—Q3 is an attempt at active play with queen's-side castling, but White has the better chances as the players rush to attack each other's king, e.g. 6 P—Q3, P—B3; 7 B—K3, B—N5; 8 QN—Q2, O—O—O; 9 R—N1, N—K2; 10 P—QN4, P—KN4; 11 P—QR4, N—N3; 12 P—N5, (Mecking *v* Korchnoi, Candidates' Match, 1974).

5...B—Q3 is an unsuccessful attempt to hold the centre with pieces rather than pawns: 6 P—Q4, B—KN5; 7 P×P, B×N; 8 Q×QB, B×P; 9 N—Q2, followed by 10 N—B4, and White has dark-square activity mentioned above.

6 P—Q4   P×P

The alternative here is 6...B—KN5; 7 P×P, Q×Q; 8 R×Q, B×N; 9 P×B, P×P; 10 B—K3, when Black has to play carefully to hold his own: 10...B—Q3 (better is 10...N—B3; 11 N—Q2, N—Q2; 12 N—B4, B—K2; 13 K—B1, R—KB1; 14 K—K2, R—B3; 15 R—Q3, R—K3; 16 QR—Q1, N—B1, with sufficient counterplay against White's doubled pawns – Markland *v* Klein, London Chess Club invitation 1973); 11 N—Q2, N—K2; 12 N—B4, O—O—O;

13 R—Q3, P—QN4; 14 N—R5, B—N5; 15 N—N3, R×R; 16 P×R, N—N3; 17 K—B1, R—B1; 18 K—K2, N—B5 ch; 19 B×N, R×B; 20 R—KN1. Although White's king's-side pawns are doubled, the better position of his king and rook gives him good endgame winning chances. The Fischer *v* Rubinetti game, Buenos Aires 1970, concluded 20...R—R5; 21 R×P, R×P; 22 P—R3, B—Q3; 23 P—B4!, P×P; 24 P—Q4, K—Q1; 25 N—R5, P—B4; 26 P—K5, B—B1; 27 N—B6 ch, K—K1; 28 R×BP, Resigns.

7 N×P   N—K2

7...P—QB4; 8 N—N3, Q×Q; 9 R×Q is analogous to the Lasker *v* Tarrasch game on page 115, and has largely been out of favour since Fischer crushed Portisch from this position at the 1966 Havana Olympiad.

8 B—K3	N—N3
9 N—Q2	B—Q3
10 N—B4	O—O
11 Q—Q3	N—K4
12 N×N	

It is almost invariably good policy for White to exchange pieces in this line; the only real exceptions to this policy are cases of exchanging on Q5 or Q6, which is normally bad since, in undoubling Black's QB pawns, White abandons his 'normal' winning chances with his king's-side majority in the ending.

| 12 . . . | B×N |
| 13 P—KB4 | B—Q3 |

187. *White to play*

14 P—B5

Normally this is not a good idea – it

makes the creation of a passed pawn on the king's side very difficult, but here it fits in well with White's middle game plans and, as it turns out, by no means adversely affects his endgame prospects.

14 . . .	Q—K2
15 B—B4	B×B
16 R×B	B—Q2
17 R—K1	Q—B4
18 P—B3	QR—K1
19 P—KN4	

White increases his stranglehold on Black's position. As the pressure mounts and king's-side attacking chances loom large, Black will be faced with the unenviable decision: to risk going under to a king's-side storm or to exchange pieces into an unfavourable endgame.

19 . . .	Q—Q3
20 Q—N3	R—K2
21 N—B3	P—B4
22 P—K5!	

Forcing open the king's file, thus creating the possibility of exchanging off all the major pieces.

22 . . .	P×P
23 R(4)—K4	B—B3
24 R×P	R(1)—K1
25 R×R	R×R
26 N—K5	P—R3
27 P—KR4	B—Q2
28 Q—B4	Q—KB3

Now White finds a way to exchange off both the remaining rooks and the queens as well.

| 29 R—K2! | B—B1 |

29...Q×RP?; 30 N—N6 wins for White.

| 30 Q—B4 ch | K—R2 |
| 31 N—N6 | R×R |

32 Q×R	B—Q2
33 Q—K7	Q×Q
34 N×Q	

188. *Black to play*

Black's king is trapped, his bishop is bad (it never even gets time to capture on N5), and White's king's-side pawn majority looks most imposing, especially the cramping pawn on KB5.

The game concluded neatly:

| 34 . . . | P—KN4 |

Black must free his king, though to do so involves the loss of a pawn.

35 P×P	P×P
36 N—Q5!	B—B3
37 N×P	B—B6

Apparently regaining the pawn, but . . .

38 N—K8	K—R3
39 N—B6	K—N2
40 K—B2	B—Q8

The king and pawn ending would be hopelessly lost for Black. Now it seems that Black must finally capture the NP. However, . . .

| 41 N—Q7! | P—B5 |

41...B×P now fails to 42 P—B6 ch, K—N1 (or 42...K—N3; 43 P—B7, K×P; 44 N—K5 ch); 43 P—B7 ch!

| 42 K—N3 | **Resigns** |

Queen's Gambit Declined—Exchange Variation

The Queen's Gambit Declined is another opening which White can choose to play with his eyes fixed firmly on his chances in the endgame, and this applies particularly to the Exchange Variation. The following game shows White treating the position in an endgame-oriented way:

Evans *v* Opsahl, Dubrovnik Olympiad 1950:
1 P—Q4, N—KB3; 2 P—QB4, P—K3; 3 N—QB3, P—Q4; 4 B—N5, QN—Q2; 5 P—K3, B—K2; 6 Q—B2, O—O; 7 P×P, P×P; 8 N—B3, P—B3; 9 B—Q3, R—K1; 10 O—O, N—B1.

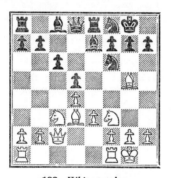

189. *White to play*

So we reach a standard position for this opening, see Diagram 189. Games from this type of position usually follow the course of White advancing on the queen's side (the well-known 'minority attack') where he hopes to create a permanent weakness which can be attacked in the endgame. Meanwhile, Black looks for counterchances on the king's side.

An underlying strength of White's strategy is that it does not depend on capturing a weak black queen's-side pawn. The worst feature of a permanent pawn weakness is that it immobilizes pieces. So, in playing the QGD Exchange Variation, White has in view endgames which can eventually resolve into the active versus passive rook situation discussed in Chapter 5.

This is what happens in the rest of the game, and White's long-winded but logical procedure can be analysed in these steps:

(*a*) White creates a permanent pawn target on the queen's side: 11 QR—N1, N—K5; 12 B×B, Q×B; 13 P—QN4, P—QR3; 14 P—QR4, N×N; 15 Q×N, B—N5; 16 N—Q2, Q—N4; 17 KR—B1, R—K3; 18 P—N5, RP×P; 19 P×P, B—R6; 20 P—N3, QR—K1; 21 P×P, P×P.

(*b*) White eliminates Black's king's-side attack by exchanges, simplifies into a clear-cut endgame, then ties down Black's rook and knight to passive defence of the weak pawn: 22 B—B1, B×B; 23 N×B, N—N3; 24 R—N6, N—K2; 25 Q—N4, P—R4; 26 R—N8, R×R; 27 Q×R ch, K—R2; 28 Q—B4, Q×Q; 29 NP×Q, P—N3; 30 N—Q2, R—Q3; 31 K—B1, K—N2; 32 R—R1, R—Q2; 33 N—N3, R—N2; 34 N—B5 R—N7; 35 R—R7, K—B3: 36 R—R6, R—N8 ch; 37 K—N2, R—N7; 38 R—R7, R—N8; 39 R—B7.

190. *Black to play*

(*c*) White probes the king's side and wins a pawn by neat tactics on that flank, while Black's defence is hampered by the need to guard the weak QBP: 39...R—QR8; 40 N—Q3, K—K3; 41 N—B5 ch, K—B3; 42 N—Q7 ch, K—K3; 43 N—B8 ch, K—B3; 44 N—R7 ch,

K—K3; 45 N—N5 ch, K—Q3; 46 R—N7, P—B3; 47 N—R7, K—K3; 48 N—B8 ch, K—B2; 49 N×P, K×N; 50 R×N.

(*d*) White makes progress in the rook ending by swapping off one of his doubled pawns: 50...K—B4; 51 R—QB7, R—QB8; 52 R—B8, K—N3; 53 K—N3, R—B8; 54 P—R4, K—B4; 55 R—KR8, K—N3; 56 P—B5 ch, K×P; 57 R×P ch.

(*e*) White mobilizes his passed KRP, utilizing the threats to exchange rooks into a pawn ending – which is always good for White because Black's 'endgame opening pawn' at QB3 is too far back to be useful in a race to queen: 57...K—N3; 58 R—R8, K—B4; 59 K—N2, R—B8; 60 R—KN8, R—QR8; 61 P—R5, R—R2; 62 R—N3, R—R2; 63 R—R3, K—N4; 64 K—B3, R—R3; 65 R—R1, K—B4; 66 K—N3, K—N4; 67 R—R4, K—B4; 68 R—B4 ch, K—N4;

69 R—N4 ch, K—B4; 70 K—R4, R—R1; 71 R—N7, R—R1; 72 P—R6, R—R8; 73 R—N3, R—R8 ch; 74 R—R3, R—KN8.

191. *White to play*

(*f*) White forces the exchange of rooks and wins the pawn ending: **75 R—B3 ch, K—N3; 76 R—N3 ch, R×R; 77 K×R, K×P; 78 K—N4, K—N3; 79 K—B4, K—N2; 80 K—B5, K—B2; 81 P—B3, Resigns.**

French Defence—Tarrasch Variation

The Tarrasch Variation of the French is another typical endgame opening in which Black has a choice of evils: a bad bishop or an isolated QP.

The problem of the bad bishop, carrying over into an ending, is seen in the following game:

Karpov *v* Hort, Budapest 1973: **1 P—K4, P—K3; 2 P—Q4, P—Q4; 3 N—Q2, N—KB3; 4 P—K5, KN—Q2; 5 P—QB3, P—QB4; 6 B—Q3, N—QB3; 7 N—K2, Q—N3; 8 N—B3, P×P; 9 P×P, P—B3; 10 P×P, N×BP; 11 O—O, B—Q3; 12 N—B3, O—O; 13 B—K3.** See Diagram 192.

Black's QB is clearly bad, hindered by its own pawns, and this situation gets worse as the game goes on.

13 . . . Q—Q1

13...Q×NP; 14 N—QN5!, is too risky.

14 B—KN5 B—Q2
15 R—K1 Q—N1

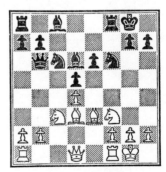

192. *Black to play*

16 B—R4! P—QR3
17 R—QB1 P—QN4

More and more of Black's pawns occupy light squares.

18 B—N1	B—B5
19 B—N3	B×B
20 RP×B	Q—N3
21 N—K2	QR—K1
22 N—B4	N×P

This pseudo-sacrifice in no way helps to alleviate the basic disadvantage of Black's position – the bad bishop; rather it helps White towards the goal he seeks of a good knight versus bad bishop endgame.

23 Q×N

23 N×N!, P—K4; 24 N×QP, Q×N!; 25 N×N ch, R×N; 26 Q×Q, P×Q; 27 R×R ch, B×R; 28 R—B8, K—B2; 29 R—Q8, as pointed out by Karpov after the game, is even better, but Karpov is concentrating on his chances in the forthcoming endgame, and the exchange of queens is a desired part of his plans.

| 23 . . . | Q×Q |
| 24 N×Q | P—K4 |

193. *White to play*

| 25 N(B4)—K6 | B×N |
| 26 R×P | |

Now Black has both a bad bishop *and* an isolated QP.

26 . . .	B—Q2
27 R×R	R×R
28 P—B3	R—QB1
29 R×R ch	B×R

Now that the rooks have gone the kings can safely be centralized.

| 30 K—B2 | K—B2 |

| 31 K—K3 | K—K2 |
| 32 P—QN4 | |

Beginning to fix Black's pawns on light squares.

| 32 . . . | P—N3 |

194. *White to play*

Every single black pawn occupies a square of the same colour as his bishop; positionally his cause is hopeless.

| 33 P—N4 | N—Q2 |
| 34 P—B4 | N—B1 |

34. . .K—Q3 immediately would have offered more resistance since then the knight could occupy the more active QN3 square.

35 P—N5	K—Q3
36 K—B3	N—K3
37 N×N	B×N

Reaching a good versus bad bishop ending which concluded: **38 K—K3, B—N5; 39 B—Q3, B—K3; 40 K—Q4, B—N5; 41 B—B2, B—K3; 42 B—N3, B—B2; 43 B—Q1, B—K3; 44 B—B3, B—B2; 45 B—N4, Resigns.** The pawn ending is lost after 45. . .B—K3; 46 B×B, K×B; 47 K—B5, and otherwise there is no other answer to the threatened B—B8.

Karpov *v* Uhlmann, Madrid 1973, shows the other side of the coin. Uhlmann chooses the isolated QP rather than the bad bishop: 1 P—K4, P—K3; 2 P—Q4, P—Q4; 3 N—Q2, P—QB4; 4 KP×P, KP×P; 5 KN—B3, N—QB3; 6 B—N5, B—Q3; 7 P×P, B×BP; 8 O—O, N—K2; 9 N—N3, B—Q3.

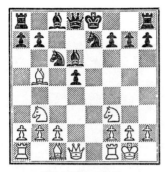

195. *White to play*

10 B—N5

The position in Diagram 195 was the subject of a remarkable theoretical battle in the Karpov *v* Korchnoi world championship candidates' match in September-November 1974. Korchnoi showed his complete faith in the black position by adopting it many times. Naturally, both he and Karpov were well aware of the endgame opening theme, so Korchnoi's play was directed towards securing a middle game with the queens still on the board and active piece play which would compensate for the latent weakness of the isolated QP and QB.

Several of the games continued from Diagram 195 (sometimes with transpositions or variations in the move order) 10 QN—Q4, O—O; 11 P—B3, B—KN5; 12 Q—R4. Korchnoi answered the queen manoeuvre first with 12...B—R4, then with 12...N×N, and finally by 12...Q—Q2. Each time he prevented Karpov from reaching the desired knight against bad bishop endgame, and after the sixth draw with 10 QN—Q4 or allied positions Karpov reverted to the move he had used against Kuzmin and Uhlmann.

10 ...   O—O
11 B—KR4

Karpov *v* Korchnoi, 18th game 1974, continued 11 R—K1, Q—B2; 12 P—B3, B—KN5; 13 P—KR3, B—R4; 14 B—K2, P—KR3; 15 B×N, N×B; 16 KN—Q4, B×B; 17 Q×B. A few moves later, Karpov succeeded in swapping a pair of

knights to reach a knight versus bishop situation – but this time Korchnoi's bishop was the 'good', dark-squared one, and the queens also remained on the board. In the sequel, White's pressure against the black QP proved insufficient for a win. As a general rule, it is better to choose active play in the middle game rather than allow yourself to be driven on to the weaker side of one of the classical endgame openings.

11 ...   B—KN5

Worse still is 11...Q—B2?; 12 B—N3, swapping off the dark-squared bishops at once (Karpov *v* Kuzmin, interzonal, Leningrad 1973) – but the reason that Karpov did not try to repeat his Kuzmin and Uhlmann successes against Korchnoi was the active variation 11...Q—N3!; 12 B—Q3, P—QR4! discovered by the Moscow master Gulko, when Black's queen's-side counterplay makes it difficult for White to carry through his strategic plan of reaching an endgame opening advantage.

12 B—K2

Black seems to have no problems with his light-squared bishop in this position, but Karpov still steers for an endgame opening situation. Play continued: 12...B—R4; 13 R—K1, Q—N3; 14 KN—Q4, B—N3; 15 P—QB3, KR—K1; 16 B—B1, B—K5; 17 B—N3, B×B; 18 RP×B, P—QR4; 19 P—QR4, N×N; 20 N×N, N—B3; 21 B—N5, KR—Q1; 22 P—KN4!, N×N; 23 Q×N, Q×Q; 24 P×Q, QR—B1.

196. *White to play*

The position looks completely level. Black has even been able to contest the QB file first; but in reality White has very much the upper hand. Black's isolated QP is no longer such a serious weakness as it is no longer on a half-open file, but Black's bishop is potentially a very bad one, especially after White's 22 P—KN4! which removed the KB4 square from use by the bishop. The rest of the game shows Karpov utilizing the bad bishop to make a decisive seventh rank penetration with his rooks: **25 P—B3, B—N3; 26 R—K7, P—N3; 27 QR—K1, P—R3; 28 R—N7, R—Q3; 29 R(1)—K7, P—R4; 30 P×P, B×P; 31** P—KN4, B—N3; 32 P—B4, R—B8 ch; 33 K—B2, R—B7 ch; 34 K—K3, B—K5; 35 R×BP, R—N3; 36 P—N5, K—R2; 37 R(B7)—K7, R×QNP; 38 B—K8, R—N6 ch; 39 K—K2, R—N7 ch; 40 K—K1, R—Q3; 41 R×P ch, K—R1; 42 R(KN7)—K7, **Resigns.** If Black meets the threatened 43 R—N8, by 42...R—Q1, then 43 P—N6 is immediately decisive (43...R—N7; 44 R—R7 ch, K—N1; 45 B—B7 ch, and 46 P—N7 ch, with mate in two moves.)

King's Indian Defence—Sämisch Variation

The Sämisch Variation is capable of at least two separate treatments; White may use the pawn on KB3 as a launching pad for a king's-side attack, or use it simply to support his centre in order to cramp Black while looking for a suitable opportunity to transpose into a favourable endgame.

The idea of playing the Sämisch as an endgame opening was used to great effect by Botvinnik in the following game:

Botvinnik *v* Tal, 13th game 1961 World Championship match: **1 P—Q4, N—KB3; 2 P—QB4, P—KN3; 3 N—QB3, B—N2; 4 P—K4, P—Q3; 5 P—B3, O—O; 6 B—K3, P—K4; 7 P×P, P×P; 8 Q×Q, R×Q.**

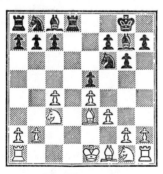

197. *White to play*

9 N—Q5	N×N
10 BP×N	P—QB3
11 B—QB4	P—QN4

Black can play 11...P×P; 12 B×QP, N—B3, leaving White with only a very small endgame advantage, but Botvinnik had calculated that Tal would be in aggressive mood in this game and that he might well take positional risks in the hope of obtaining tactical chances that he could turn to advantage.

| 12 B—N3 | B—N2 |
| 13 O—O—O | P—QB4 |

'It was on this very move that White was counting, although it looks inconsistent. Of course Black ought not to leave White with a protected passed pawn which also restricts his queen's bishop.' This note and subsequent quoted notes in the game are all by Botvinnik.

See Diagram 198.

| 14 B—QB2 |

'Here it is not difficult to find a plan... (it) consists of preparing to undermine Black's pawn chain by P—QN3 and P—QR4. It is surprising that although

198. *White to play*

White was clearly aiming at carrying out this plan, my opponent did not try to counter it.'

One possible reason for Tal's failure to counter Botvinnik's plan is that it is an *endgame* plan, and although White is very definitely thinking in terms of the ending it is quite possible that Black, after only fourteen moves of an aggressive defence, was thinking solely in terms of the middle game. This represents an important psychological advantage to those who can plan in terms of the endgame opening.

14 . . .	N—Q2
15 N—K2	B—KB1
16 N—B3	P—QR3

"Possibly the losing move. Black's bishop will now remain out of play for a long time and, what is more important, White realizes his plan without any

hindrance. Black should have decided on 16. . .P—N5.'

17 P—QN3	QR—B1
18 B—Q3	N—N3
19 B—K2	R—Q3
20 K—N2	P—B4

'After 20. . .P—N5; 21 N—N1, P—B5; 22 P×P, N×P ch; 23 B×N, R×B; 24 R—QB1, White penetrates along the QB file.'

21 R—QB1	R—KB3
22 P—QR4	NP×P
23 NP×P	P—QR4

'23. . .P—QB5; 24 K—B2, B—N5; 25 R—QN1, B×N; 26 B×N, (or 26 K×B, N×RP ch; 27 K—B2) would make no difference.' But now White is clearly winning; his two trumps are the QN file and, after further simplification, the passed QP.

The game concluded:

24 K—B2, P—QB5; 25 R—QN1, B—N5; 26 N—R2, B—B4; 27 B×B, R×B; 28 N—B3, B—B1; 29 R—N2, B—Q2; 30 KR—QN1, B×P ch; 31 N×B, N×N; 32 R—N8 ch, K—N2; 33 R(1)—N7 ch, R—KB2; 34 P—Q6, R×R; 35 R×R ch, K—B3; 36 R×P, R—B1; 37 P—Q7, R—Q1; 38 B×P, N—B4; 39 R—B7 ch, K—N4; 40 B—N5, P×P; 41 P×P, Resigns. White's QP costs Black his knight.

English Opening

Here again there are lines involving an early exchange of queens which can almost be regarded as endgames from move six or seven.

One example: 1 P—QB4, N—KB3; 2 N—QB3, P—KN3; 3 N—B3, P—Q4; 4 P×P, N×P; 5 P—K4, N×N; 6 QP×N, Q×Q ch; 7 K×Q, and White stands a little better for the ensuing endgame. See Diagram 199.

In the game Hort v Smejkal, Prague, 1972, play continued: 7. . .B—N2; 8 K—B2, N—Q2; 9 B—KB4, P—QB3;

10 N—Q2, O—O; 11 P—B3, P—KB4; 12 B—KN5, B—B3; 13 B×B, N×B; 14 B—B4 ch, K—N2; 15 P—K5, N—K1; 16 QR—Q1, N—B2; 17 N—N3, P—B5; 18 K—B1, B—B4; 19 R—Q2, QR—Q1.

White's advantage in Diagram 200 will seem microscopic to the average player, but is typical of the situation for

199. *Black to play*

which a grandmaster aims when he chooses an endgame opening. White's knight has potential outposts at QR5, QB5, and Q4, while his bishop and KP form a central barricade. Finally, White can control the only open file. In Diagram 200, he has the possibility of: 20 N—Q4, B—B1; 21 KR—Q1, N—Q4; 22 N—B2, B—K3; 23 N—N4, with a clear advantage. Instead Hort prefers a more complex sacrificial idea which leads to an ending with imbalance of

200. *White to play*

material and good chances for White.

Play continued: 20 KR—Q1, R×R; 21 R×R, P—KN4; 22 N—R5, B—B1; 23 N×NP!, B×N; 24 R—Q7, B—R3; 25 R×P ch, K—R1; 26 B×B, N×B. Now White played 27 P—QN4? and lost after further mistakes. He had good chances to clinch his opening endgame strategy after 27 R×QRP, e.g. 27...N—B4; 28 K—B2, R—Q1; 29 P—QR4, N—Q6; 30 P—R5, N—K8 ch (or 30... N×KP; 31 P—R6, P—B4; 32 R—QB7, P—B5; 33 R—B5!, R—K1; 34 P—R7 etc.); 31 K—N3, P—N5; 32 P—R6, followed by 33 R—QN7, 34 P—R7, and 35 R—N8.

Sicilian Defence

Few players with the white pieces against the Sicilian Defence consider aiming for the endgame; after all, it is widely known that White's normal policy is king's-side attack, while Black tries for counter-chances along the QB file. However, there are three major situations where endgame opening strategy is important in the Sicilian.

(a) Black tries to counter the standard king's-side attack by simplification.

A popular example of this occurs in the Yugoslav Attack: 1 P—K4, P—QB4; 2 N—KB3, P—Q3; 3 P—Q4, P×P; 4 N×P, N—KB3; 5 N—QB3, P—KN3; 6 B—K3, B—N2; 7 P—B3, N—B3; 8 Q—Q2, O—O; 9 B—QB4, N×N; 10 B×N, B—K3; 11 B—N3, Q—R4; 12 O—O—O. See Diagram 201.

In the early days of this type of position, White used to go crudely forward on the king's side with P—KN4 and P—KR4, while Black pushed

his QNP. Experience showed that the outcome was most uncertain, and so White's attention switched to simplifying by K—N1 and N—Q5. This in itself does not lead to a won ending, but the discovery which caused the variation to be assessed as better for White was that in some of the endgames White can achieve a mobile 2–1 queen's-side pawn majority by enticing Black's QNP to the fifth rank before initiating wholesale swaps.

201. *Black to play*

Analysis of a critical line goes: **12. . . P—QN4; 13 K—N1, KR—B1; 14 KR— K1, B×B; 15 BP×B, P—N5; 16 B×N!, P×N; 17 B×BP, B×B; 18 P×B, R× P; 19 R—K3, R(1)—QB1; 20 R×R, Q×R; 21 Q×Q, R×Q; 22 R—QB1, R×R ch; 23 K×R.**

Now the king and pawn ending is won for White.

202. *Black to play*

The finish could be: **23. . .K—B1; 24 K—B2, K—K1; 25 K—B3, K—Q2; 26 K—B4, K—B3; 27 P—QN4, P—K3; 28 P—N4, P—N4; 29 P—N5 ch, K—N3; 30 K—N4, P—B3; 31 P—KR3, P— KR3; 32 P—R3, K—B2; 33 K—R5, K— N2; 34 P—QR4, K—N1; 35 P—N6,** and wins.

(b) White is able to break open the centre early on and force the exchange of queens.

This endgame opening idea is the theoretical basis of the Levenfish Attack: **1 P—K4, P—QB4; 2 N—KB3, P—Q3; 3 P—Q4, P×P; 4 N×P, N—KB3; 5 N—QB3, P—KN3; 6 P—B4, N—B3. 6. . .B—N2;** is playable despite **7 P— K5. 7 N×N, P×N; 8 P—K5, P×P.** Black should prefer the more complex **8. . .N—Q2;** or **8. . .N—N5. 9 Q×Q ch,** **K×Q; 10 P×P, N—N5; 11 B—KB4, B—KN2; 12 O—O—O ch, B—Q2; 13 P—K6, P×P; 14 N—K4, P—K4; 15 B—K2!.**

After White's last move (a recommendation of Heidenfeld) he will soon regain the sacrificed pawn when Black is left with a wrecked pawn front for the endgame.

(c) Black counter-attacks prematurely with . . . P—Q4.

In this situation, White may be able to liquidate in the centre and transpose into an ending where his 3–2 queen's-side majority is combined with threats to the black QRP and/or QNP.

This idea is shown clearly and convincingly in the following game, Bellin *v* Singleton, Middlesex League, 1973: **1 P—K4, P—QB4; 2 N—KB3, P— K3; 3 P—Q4, P×P; 4 N×P, N—KB3; 5 N—QB3, P—Q3; 6 P—KN4, B—K2; 7 P—N5, KN—Q2; 8 B—K3, N—QB3; 9 P—KR4, N—N3; 10 R—KN1, P— Q4; 11 P×P, N×P; 12 N×N(Q5),** **Q×N; 13 N×N, Q×N; 14 Q—Q4, B— Q2. If 14. . .O—O; 15 O—O—O,** Black cannot develop properly because **15. . . R—Q1;** is refuted by **16 Q×R ch. 15 Q×NP, O—O—O; 16 O—O—O, Q— R5; 17 Q—Q4, Q×RP; 18 Q×P, Q×Q; 19 B×Q, B—QB3.** See Diagram 203.

In the last few moves of this game, White switches to the king's side and wins there rather than, as expected, on the other flank. Yet this switch itself shows how the endgame opening theme may be present in the sharpest and most

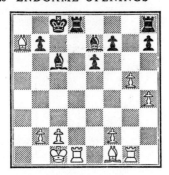

203. *White to play*

uncompromising systems of attack. White's plan, begun with 6 P—KN4, is mainly a middle game idea, intending to overwhelm Black in the centre and on the king's side if Black fails to counter actively. But it is also a manoeuvre which semi-fixes the black king's-side pawns on the second rank. If Black decides to seek relief from the middle game threats by exchanges in the centre, then these king's-side pawns are vulnerable. The exchanges will either leave the white bishops free to direct operations from the centre, as in the game above, or else will give the white rooks chances to penetrate to the seventh rank via the Q file.

The game concluded:

20 R× R ch, B× R; 21 B—Q4, R—N1; 22 B—Q3, P—B3; 23 B× RP, R—N2; 24 P—N6, B—B6; 25 B—K3, and White **Resigned.**

Diagram 203 thus shows in microcosm the underlying theme of this entire book. The endgame is not an isolated aspect of chess, but a phase for which experienced tournament players plan from a very early stage. The writer's forecast is that pioneering techniques like the Fischer endgame, the Petrosian endgame, and the endgame opening, will all grow in status as their ideas are absorbed, not just as at present by a few grandmasters and international regulars, but by hundreds and thousands of club, tournament, and postal players. And, hopefully, the practical ideas presented in *How to Play the Endgame in Chess* will enable such players to make full use of the endgame as a winning weapon at the chessboard.